MANAGING IN THE MIDDLE

Practical rules, ideas and entrepreneurial lessons for Junior and Middle Managers

by

Iain Johnston

Contact Iain at

Thefixer953@gmail.com

2014 Edition

Copyright © 2014 Iain Johnston

Illustrations by Martinus Van Tee
http://www.martinusvantee.com/

Cover design by the Loud Group

www.loudgroup.co.za

Production by
Rick Smith Books & Publishing

www.ricksmithbooks.com

Preface

There are many books on management that cover every aspect of management principles and skills development. So what makes this one different?

This is not a technical book on management principles and theory. It is about practical concepts and ideas to improve your skills, and assist you in managing the three aspects around which your organization (and in particular, your role as a manager) revolves; namely, your business, your customer, and your people.

Throughout this book, I have drawn on my experience in business, from thirty years in management and business development, and also as a pilot. I hope by sharing them with you that these proven rules and principles will assist in contributing to your success, on your journey as a manager.

There is an Eastern saying; *"The teacher and the taught, together, create the teaching."* By using just one of the ideas from this book, we will both have created a teaching moment that contributes to your never-ending improvement and development, as *The Fixer* who manages in the middle.

Sometimes it's just about doing the small things very well, instead of trying to manage a number of big things and not doing any of them well. Being a manager means you have to fix things. You may have to repair customer relationships, reconnect the links between the people on your team, and perhaps even unblock some of the channels of communication that flow between the business leaders, the customers, and the workforce.

"In our constant search for knowledge and understanding, we need to rationally sift through and remove the complexities of the influences that surround us to enable us to reveal the answers that will naturally prevail through the simplicity of our own self-induced wisdom."

Iain Johnston, August 2014

About the Author

Born in Scotland, and now based in South Africa, Iain Johnston is well known as a highly effective Management Consultant, Trainer, and Speaker with more than 30 years' experience at the sharp-end of management and business development.

Iain's passion is working in two critical business areas; Management Development, particularly junior and middle managers, where Iain and his team deliver high-value skills-based programs to accelerate management performance, and employee engagement, the key ingredient to ensure performance, productivity, and organisational effectiveness.

You can connect with Iain by e-mail at **thefixer953@gmail.com**, or on Social Media, via the links at the back of the book.

Iain Johnston

Table of Contents

Iain Johnston

1

What's It All About?

As a manager, do you find yourself squeezed in the middle? Do you have to deal with information and instructions dropping down from above, as well as having to retrieve and decipher information from below? We live in a world driven and controlled by technology. As a manager, do you feel you are evolving fast enough to keep up with this technology, or do you sometimes feel that technology is managing you?

One may argue that the most important person in your business, be it a large corporation, medium sized, or small business, is the CEO, MD, or business owner. Yes, they provide the direction, strategy, and, very importantly, "inspirational leadership," but the most important person in your business is YOU, the manager in the middle!

Why? Well, you are in the middle of what I call the BCE triangle: the triangle that organizational behavior revolves around. The three sides of the triangle are the BUSINESS (represented by the CEO, MD, or business owner), the CUSTOMER, and the EMPLOYEES (the people who make up your organization). The representatives of the three sides of this triangle all have their own needs and objectives, or what is called their "WHAT'S IN IT FOR ME?" In other words:

- The BUSINESS leaders want performance and results.
- The CUSTOMERS want great products, service, and value.
- The EMPLOYEES want their needs to be met at work.

Remember, when dealing with people, and despite the sophistication of communication, their basic needs, irrespective of which side of the triangle they are on, are to simply be understood, respected, appreciated, and have their self-interests addressed.

Traditionally, the flow is from the top-down: leaders wanting better performance and results. Businesses are constantly looking at ways of managing customer relationships as well as continually managing and motivating people. As a manager in the middle of this BCE triangle, you are the important link because of the responsibility you have managing the execution of the BUSINESS plan. You control the outcomes through your ability to manage, direct, and engage every single team member to ensure you meet the expectations of your CUSTOMERS as well as the task of facilitating and meeting the needs of the EMPLOYEE. You are required to manage all the technical as well as "people" related issues and challenges that are part of everyday business.

In this book we will look at how you, as a manager in the middle, can reverse the top-down approach to a bottom-up approach, through understanding and facilitating the needs of the EMPLOYEE, who is engaged in meeting the needs and expectations of the CUSTOMER, who, in turn, delivers and meets the needs of the LEADERS. This means better business performance.

In the world at large, and in your business in particular, it is all about change: a word we hear every day and is as inevitable as the sun rising in the east and setting in the west. You need to change as managers, and the people you manage certainly need to change too. Some embrace this change, while others don't. Your success will rest on your ability to manage this change. Sometimes, despite all odds, people will not move from their position, so you may have to do things differently.

A main part of the changes we experience are in the area of technology. It drives business today and adds to the influences and complexities of your world of managing in the middle. These influences and complexities can and do distract; and as a result, you feel frustrated and even vulnerable when the pressures and expectations from above and below are applied.

Don't let technology manage you. As a manager in the middle, you want to let technology do what technology does, and let people do what people do.

As a junior or middle manager, you will receive a constant stream of feedback through comments, criticisms, instructions, complaints, requests, disruptions, and problems from your senior management and the people on your team as well as your customers. It will come at you from all angles, and being a manager in the middle, there is nowhere to hide and no way of predicting where it will come from next. Some of this feedback will be good; some will cast doubts in your mind and cause you to question your decisions and actions.

Changing your direction every time you get this feedback will throw you off course and affect your decisions, and consequently, the way you manage. So to be the best at managing in the middle, do not waste your time on things you cannot control. Instead, concentrate on yourself, your skills, your knowledge, your determination, and the plotting and execution of your plan that will take you to your destination.

There is a law that controls everything we do in business and life. It is called the law of cause and effect, which originated around 410 BC with the Greek philosopher Socrates. He spoke about the reasons things happen, the causes and effects of our lives, and the process of achievement toward future goals and objectives. Known as the Socrates law of causality, the law of cause and effect simply means that for every effect (result) in your life, there was a specific cause (action) that led to that effect. If you focus on these actions steps one at a time instead of trying to influence the end results, things become easier to manage. It is a useful law to keep in mind when you find the result is not what you wanted or expected. Check the actions that led to the result and see if you can find the step you need to correct. We will discuss a simple rule that will help you.

The way we think and act is a process. Like building a house, it starts with an idea or concept. This idea is translated into a plan or drawing, and the house is built brick by brick from the foundation up. Managing requires you to do things in sequence in order to achieve the desired effect. It is this systematic and habitual implementation of systems and processes that I will refer to in the book as *keeping in step*. *Keeping in step* means keeping or maintaining a rhythm or timing through practice, just as a soldier or dancer would do. Through practicing each move or step, their routines are perfected.

As a manager, the truth is that one of the most important things we need to understand is that needs drive behavior and not necessarily your managerial influence. We like to think we are in control, only to find there are some things in life we cannot control: one of them being people's behavior. As a manager new to this role, this can be a very frustrating thing and one which many new managers never really come to terms. As we explore the life of a manager in this book, we will see that the key to becoming a good manager lies in your ability to understand needs and how you can combine this understanding with your managerial skills, knowledge, and influence.

What influences are you subjected to each day? What unexpected rush of events blow in? Which way is the wind blowing? As a manager, you will be responsible for the delivery of one or a combination of key business performance areas; namely,

- Increase and improve revenue

- Increase profitability

- Improve organizational effectiveness

- Manage or decrease expenses

These performance areas are the pressure points in managing in the middle. These are your pain points, and the constant and incessant need to meet the numbers is what your business revolves around. Everything you and your team are engaged in will pivot around these areas. In addition, you may be facing other pressures and expectations.

For example:

1. Immediate and senior management: this may be your MD in a smaller business environment or a GM or director in a bigger corporate environment. Here the pressure comes from meeting budgets, managing expenses, employee engagement, and general business expectations.

2. The environment: the company and business environment, your personal and financial situation, and the market conditions.

3. People: the individuals on your team, business unit, branch or division that fall under your management, and their expectations, issues, concerns and demands.

4. You: your ambitions, desires, dreams, goals, and future, and the historical journey you have been on to get to this point as a manager.

Who wins the tug of war? Which of these influences have the most impact on what you do as a manager, and what percentage of your day is spent across these areas? How do you separate or prioritize when you are caught in the center of these influences? Depending on your level of management, one may have more importance or influence than the others.

You may sometimes be faced with what seems to be an impossible task. Everything you see in front of you is confusing and perhaps a little intimidating, and you wonder if you are ever going to be able to do it or get it right. Let me give you an example.

Many years ago, I got my private pilot's license: a dream I had from a very young age. On the first flight I had with my instructor, I sat in the cockpit of this small Piper training airplane, took one look at the instruments, switches, and controls and thought, "How on earth am I going to be able to fly this airplane!" Well, of course, once we took off, the fear and uncertainty were magnified and even more so when I took over the controls. Understandably, I was erratic, and after I landed, I realized my shirt was soaked. The concentration in that short first flight left me with a headache, but at the same time exhilarated!

On January 22, 1984, I took to the skies on my first solo flight. The certificate I was presented with after this flight said:

> *"Let it be known to all men and ground bound creeping things that upon this day, the 22nd January 1984, I Johnston has duly completed a memorable first solo flight, and this certificate serves to mark this auspicious event and to bear witness to the skill and precision of the holder who, nothing daunted, did clatter off into the blue, circumnavigate the airfield, and land gaily, proving that the age of miracles is not yet dead."*

> *Given my hand, albeit, shaky………… Instructor*

What would the words be when you have successfully navigated the world of managing in the middle?

Something like this perhaps?

This certificate serves to mark the auspicious event and to bear witness to the SKILL and precision of the holder who, as a manager in the middle, nothing daunted, did master the difficulties of managing the business in the middle, circumnavigated the turbulence and winds of change, and gaily achieved the required business objectives and successful ORGANIZATIONAL EFFECTIVENESS, proving that the age of miracles is not yet over."

Learning to fly is, of course, the same as learning to drive a car: a systematic approach and step-by-step process to develop understanding and competencies. The only difference is that you can't pull over to the side of the road and take a short break! As a pilot, you have to make decisions based on what you see in the cockpit (your business) and outside the aircraft (your market place). As you will see, the rules and principles we will discuss in the following chapters are the basis of what managing in the middle is about.

I made significant progress from that first flight with the instructor to being able to fly my first solo flight circuit of the airfield on my own. I still had a long way to go before I attained my pilot's license, but I had taken a significant first step. It was a definite step that allowed me to **see not where I still had to go, but where I had started from and what had been accomplished**. This is a key principle to managing in the middle, as it was through my learning to fly. It was from my flying experience, and in fact, a mistake I had made, that some of the rules of managing in the middle evolved.

How do I get across the river?

Have you ever sat on the bank of a river and watched a sun set or just took in the flow of the water and attuned yourself to the sounds around you?

These are the times when you are free of the surrounding clutter that normally fills and distracts your everyday business life, and your mind is free of interruption, and you are open to moments of inspiration.

Sitting there, watching the river, do you find yourself wondering how you would get to the other side and what route you would take as you look for rocks and exposed areas that you could use as footholds? As a manager, it's a similar view when looking at your business and knowing you need to manage your team to achieve your goals and objectives; you always need to be looking for the best way to cross your river.

Throughout the world, there is a diversity of climatic conditions from tropical forest regions to arid deserts and mountain ranges; there are also many rivers and streams ranging from the mighty river to small localized rivers and streams. Through the seasons, these rivers and streams can range from being a dry riverbed during the dry season to raging torrents of water in the wet season.

You will be faced with obstacles, challenges, and day-to-day situations that need to be managed in order to achieve your business objectives: the things you need to deal with in order to get to the other side of your river. Crossing rivers is unpredictable, and if flowing strongly, can be hazardous. The state of the river, like your environment as a manager, is subjected to the droughts and thunderstorms that can change this landscape overnight.

You may experience days where managing in the middle is like a dry riverbed. Initially this may seem an easy journey across a bed covered in a spider web of hard, cracked mud, but underneath this seemingly dry mud lies a softer, more liquid mud, and by stepping through this crust, this treacherous mud will slow you down.

You will have days when getting to the other side of your river is easy. You and your team will enjoy a moment of engagement and synergy and will not be dragged down by any obstacles or circumstances. Then there will be days when simply crossing a dry riverbed proves to be a challenge.

Managing in the middle is often as if standing on the bank of a fast-flowing river with rapids of swirling and cascading water rushing over rocks and branches, and debris flowing and bobbing in the water as it is caught up in the swift current of the river. The river may be wide, and the water temperature may vary from tropical warmth to icy cold caused from the recently melted snow in the surrounding mountains.

Crossing this river requires planning, communication, concentration, and team work. With this river, all you can see in front of you is the murky water with no apparent way across and no visible or easy support system in place for you to hold onto.

You are, of course, surrounded by technology, which impacts every part of your life. For the most part, technology assists us positively in many different ways, but it can also impact negatively or adversely on how we manage people.

Manager in the middle notes:

When something initially seems too difficult, break it down into little steps or actions, and step by step, you will achieve the desired effect.

The three sides of the BCE triangle are made up of people who want their needs met. Don't let the winds they create cause so much turbulence that you are detracted and constantly blown off course from your key responsibility as a manager.

Action step: Measure what you have achieved by looking at where you started and *what* has been accomplished, not by where you still have to go. Celebrate each step.

Summary: Understand the business performance area you need to focus on:

- Increase and improve revenue

- Increase profitability

- Improve organizational effectiveness. Always look for the opportunities that will develop the synergy between the organization, the customer, and the employees. That is what creates organizational effectiveness.

- Manage or decrease expenses

Concentrate on how to cross your river. What is the step or obstacle you need to deal with first? The quickest way to get to the other side is not always in a straight line.

"Success comes from doing the small things very well all the time."

2

Whatever Happened to "Keep It Simple?"

Has business truly become too technical and complex? Have we reached the point of no return?

Evolving with technology can be a full-time job. The speed at which new applications, software, and hardware devices are introduced is frenetic. Competence and technical aptitude vary from those who are managers in IT and closer to the stream of new developing technology to the more mainstream managers in sales, marketing, and operations where competency is in using the technology with smart phone applications and software office suites on laptops. It's what we do with the technology: more specifically, what we do with the information it gives us. Can we balance the technology and still "Keep in Step?" In other words, can we balance technology with the way we manage by practicing each step of our routines to maintain rhythm and consistency?

While speaking with a few people in management positions in industries ranging from retail to medical, I asked if they thought they could make their day-to-day lives simpler. They said, "Yes, but it's not an easy thing to do. There is so much going on and so much time spent in administration, reports, and number crunching. Time is something we don't seem to have." TIME MANAGEMENT may make you more efficient, but ACTIVITY MANAGEMENT will make you more effective.

In contrast to what these managers had to say about their day-to-day managerial world, when senior managers were asked what their challenges and frustrations were, their answers were **execution**: people not always executing their duties; **productivity**: not always getting things done or taking longer to do than they should (execution); and constantly dealing with **"people"** issues like motivation and conflict that take up a lot of time and energy when they should be focusing on more important things.

So the main issues and challenges that senior management face can be packaged under one umbrella: "chasing and making the numbers." Conversely, as junior and middle management, you have to deal with the constantly changing winds that blow from all directions, and you feel as if you are in the eye of the storm. As soon as you move in any direction, you will be swept away by these surrounding prevailing winds.

Your business comprises of two main elements: **technology** that measures and provides you with information in various shapes and forms, and **the people** that make up your team and the organizational structure of your organization, both of which you, as the manager in the middle, need to manage. Technology requires little interaction, and apart from you having to learn the skill of understanding how it works, it does what you program it to do. People, on the other hand, require a considerable amount of interaction and don't come with an instruction manual, but you are required to develop the skill of understanding how they work, a skill we will discuss in the chapter on employee engagement. Einstein had this to say about technology:

"I fear the day that technology will surpass our human interaction. The world will have a generation of idiots."

Now before you throw your hands into the air in disbelief, especially if you are in information technology, let's look at the definition of the word "idiot." The word comes from the ancient Greek meaning a person lacking in professional skills (in context, a person who did not pursue public office) and characterized by self-centeredness. Einstein was alluding to the fact that if people become so engrossed in what they see and do using technology, they will become very self-centered and lose their ability to engage in "public affairs," which is people engagement.

Today the word has evolved in the English language to mean something different from the original context in which it was used, and its translation, as I am sure applies to all languages around the world, means a foolish or stupid person.

As a manager, you are under pressure to perform, to manage your department, to *fix* things, and to arrive at your end goal, whatever that may be. It's all about productivity, which is a measure of your success as a manager. Keep checking your own productivity as well as your team, department, or group. Is it up or down, and if so, why?

It is interesting that the 80/20 principle applies, as it does to so many things in our lives, to the meetings you have with your team. Test this principle the next time you have a meeting, and you will see that, statistically, decisions are made in 20% of the time. The other 80% of the time is spent on discussion, most of which is unnecessary information and detail. This means that in a one hour meeting, twelve minutes will be used in making the decision, and the other forty-eight minutes will be used for discussion to get to that point!

Another useful rule to use with your team is this one. In business, you will not always agree on things. Everyone has their own ideas and suggestions. In order to manage the situation, and more importantly, come to a decision, adopt the 70/30 rule, which means 70% consensus and 100% commitment. If 70% of you agree on a decision, then everyone embraces it and gives 100% commitment to the execution. This system works well because, like all things in life, sometimes you win, and sometimes you lose. This commitment ensures you are all on the same wavelength, and more importantly, you all engage and have the same message.

For some managers, gauging the level of productivity of the people around them and the group or team as a whole may be easier if there is some sort of measurement in place. For the most part, it can be subjective. Perhaps in a recent performance review, you discovered some people were not performing. Sales results indicated their non-performance, or it may be a general feeling or indication of their reluctance to complete a task, or they constantly complain, or disengage from team or group involvement.

Productivity is the measurement of how successful you are at "crossing the river." Success is not necessarily determined by the speed in crossing the river, but more by the deliberate steps you take and the avoidance of unnecessary deviations that take you off course.

If we look at sales, for example, the activity a salesperson engages in every day will determine the success they have. Structured and focused activity will result in successful sales. General misguided activity that lacks direction and purpose very seldom produces results.

I recently went on a trip to the Arctic Circle and was in a small town in the northern part of Norway, where we went on a sled ride across the frozen lakes and arctic wilderness. There were ten Huskies harnessed in, and to watch these Huskies perform was fantastic.

As you can imagine, it is important to ensure all the dogs work together; they need to be in sync and pull together in the same direction. If two dogs are not performing, the burden of pulling the sled falls on the other eight dogs. The net effect is these dogs get tired quicker and take longer to get to the destination.

In your sales organization or team, how many of the people are not pulling their weight? What burden is being placed on the rest of the team to produce the results, and how does that affect your timeline to deliver the sales results?

Imagine that an old-fashioned scale is on your desk. On one side is the team's performance and productivity, and on the other side is the budget or project you are managing. What does the scale look like? Is it leaning, or is it perfectly balanced? If it is not balanced, what do you need to add or remove? Whatever function, area of responsibility, or link your department has in your company or organization's chain, you will have a required outcome, target, objective, and/or budget. Put that onto the scale. What balance do you need to put on the other side? This visualization is critical to your management in the middle.

What is the balance you have at the moment? Technology, measurement, systems, and processes on one side and people and results on the other? I don't know what balance you need to have in your business or in your situation, but given where you are at the moment, you need to balance the issues, challenges, frustrations, requirements to meet targets, your objectives, and even more importantly, your and your team's needs. The latter ultimately is a measurement of the level of engagement you and your team have and will determine and affect your ability to get to the other side.

Keeping in step is about being able to "rationally sift through and remove the complexities of the influences that surround us." It's not difficult to load the scale. What becomes the challenge for you as the manager is balancing the scales through the process of understanding the areas and levels of productivity. Some are visual and quite obvious. Some, unfortunately, are not that obvious. In the following chapters, we will look at the formulas you can use.

There was a recent video clip posted on social media of Admiral Bill McRavens. He was giving a graduation ceremony speech at the University of Texas. He offered his words of wisdom to these graduates as they were about to begin their business lives. Based on his military career, he had ten poignant steps to influencing and keeping it simple in the acts we do. The first one was to make your bed every day: a very mundane job in the military, but one that needs to be done correctly.

The message in this simple act of making your bed every day is that by doing it, you have accomplished the first task of the day. It's a small, yet significant, step that leads to the next one and results in completing a number of tasks (the actions) that have a significant impact on your successfully attainment of your desired results. It reinforces that the simple things in life are what matter, not the smoke and mirrors or irrelevant clutter that ends up surrounding us every day and prevents us from seeing what we need to see.

The message is simple. If you want to change the world, start off by making your bed! Fix the small things first, and the more difficult things will become so much easier to manage.

Once you establish a routine and discipline for what needs to be done, you will find some of the tasks may not be pleasant, but they are necessary. Brian Tracy, in his book "Eat the Frog," talks about doing the things we need to do and how we avoid doing them because they are not always things we like to do. Instead, he suggests "eating the frog," — doing these unpleasant but necessary things and not leaving them until tomorrow or the last moment. We do things in life for two reasons. One is to derive pleasure, and the other is to avoid pain. We, unfortunately, have to balance our own scale and sometimes do the not-so-pleasant tasks and do them first.

Performance appraisals are regularly conducted today as a means of understanding performance and using this understanding to develop people. I remember the first 360 degree performance review I had where I was subjected to what is commonly termed "constructive criticism," but today, it's described as feedback! Until that point, I considered myself to be a good manager—albeit self-proclaimed. I came from a background as a business owner and shareholder where I was "the boss" and sometimes, inadvertently, a little autocratic and dogmatic. With the benefit of hindsight, I can look back and see the level of inexperience I had in managing people.

At the conclusion of the performance review, for someone not used to this type of feedback, it was a reality check: not because of the way the review was conducted, but realizing how others saw me and the impact my management style had on other people. There are, and have been over the years, many "self-help" books written including such classics as "The Richest Man in Babylon" by George S. Clason and "Think and Grow Rich" by Napoleon Hill. "Psycho Cybernetics" by Maxwell Maltz (edited and updated by Dan S Kennedy) was one book that resonated with me. It was the term **self-image** that Maxwell Maltz used. He is credited as the first researcher and author to explain the term **self-image** and its ability to positively or negatively influence the outcome of our objectives or aspirations.

He goes on to discuss the workings of our brains: what is commonly termed our conscious and subconscious mind. It is the thoughts we have created in our conscious mind that are filtered through our *self–image* lens that dictate the automated processing by our subconscious mind, thereby creating our actions and behavior.

There is a great deal of information available on this subject, and it puts the way you think into perspective. Each piece of information is one more piece of the puzzle that forms your managerial picture.

Have you ever painted a mental picture of yourself as a manager, either as you see yourself now or as you would like to be? After my initial performance review, that's what I did. Looking back, it was a little vague in some areas, but in others, I came quite close: particularly in the way I worked with my team but sometimes missed the mark when I became impatient or intolerant. These occasions only served to remind me of my vulnerability, and that being a good manager is always a work in progress.

Take a moment and try to paint a picture in your mind of how you would like to be portrayed as a manager.

Imagine this picture as a jigsaw puzzle with missing pieces that might be from the center of the picture, or from the framework, and represent the skills and knowledge blocks you lack as a young or new manager, or they could be from the section that represents your team, people skills, and/or your management style. If so, make a note of them using a three or four word sentence describing that missing piece.

One of the missing pieces may be about prioritizing your "to do" list, and an equally important "not to do" list; both can be likened to making your bed each morning. It sets the scene, gets you to take the first step, and creates the impetus or platform to achieving bigger and better things.

Each day, the river crossing begins with the painting of a picture. What objectives are you or your team facing? As a manager, you also need to understand what every single member of your team personally faces. What do they visualize when you tell them to paint their picture? What do they see and understand, and does their picture look a little like yours? We can only see the world from our own eyes. The moment we try to decide what someone else's picture should look like, we enter the world of perception, assumption, and dare I say, frustration.

So how do you start to form some pictures in other people's minds: by telling a story!

Justin Cohen, renowned author on human potential, gives some great advice about how to tell stories as a manager.

> *"As a manager, have you ever tried to sell, persuade, or teach and noticed your audience's eyes glazing over? Perhaps you were in the audience, and the presenter had just clicked the fortieth slide. You know the one I mean: the one with twelve bullet points and a triple bar graph that you could never quite understand. The presenter finishes up and is satisfied that he or she has covered all the information. And that is exactly what the presenter has done—covered it—forgetting that the point is to uncover it!*
>
> *The most lethal bullet ever invented is called the bullet point: it will kill you with boredom. As a professional speaker, I have seen more than my fair share of these types of presentations. A company spends hundreds of thousands of dollars on an annual conference—the most important and expensive sales call of the year—and their CEO transforms into a CES: Chief Executive Soporific."*

As a manager, do you want to wake up an audience? Drop the data overload and tell a "Living Story." All communications are a form of storytelling that give an account of events, but there are two very different kinds of stories. They may say the same thing, but they have a vastly different impact on our brains.

Story number one is bland and abstract. It's what I call a "dead story." For example:

It is very important that even young people have good medical insurance to cover any hospital expenses that may arise. An illness may be unexpected, and if one doesn't have sufficient funds available, one may be faced with both medical and financial problems. Everyone should have medical insurance. Riveting stuff, huh? That's what I call a "Dead Story," and it doesn't activate much of the brain other than the part that processes language.

Story number two follows traditional storytelling. It's what I call a "Living Story." For example:

My friend Howard was fit, active, and just twenty-four years old when his doctor told him, "You've got cancer." He shook his head in disbelief, not realizing, it was about to get worse. "We need to get you into a good private hospital now. How are you going to pay?" That's when Howard put his head in his hands and started crying. As a young, healthy guy, he'd just never seen the point of having medical insurance. Fortunately, after several months of treatment, he got better, but to pay his medical costs, he had to sell his apartment. Four years later, he's still living with his parents.

Which of those two stories is more likely to motivate you to get medical insurance? Well, for the answer to that, let's see what happened in your brain when you read the second one.

31

Most likely, you made a mental image (a picture) of the whole scenario (visual cortex). You heard Howard's doctor say "cancer" (auditory cortex). You probably felt some of Howard's terror (limbic system). Then, by giving you a character in a story to identify with, your **mirror neuron network** was activated. This is the part of our brain that enables us to experience what others are going through as if we were going through it ourselves. Finally, your hippocampus fired up as a memory was laid down in your brain.

Living stories don't tell us what to think or do. They take us on journeys in someone else's shoes. They give us experiences that allow us to draw our own conclusions. Have you noticed lessons are much more powerful when we figure them out ourselves?

Furthermore, the more sensory and emotional the information is, the more likely we will remember and act. When you hear ten facts, you're lucky if you remember one. Whereas, if you hear a good story, you're likely to remember most, if not all of them.

What's the best-selling book of all time? It's called the Bible, and it's a collection of stories. Our ancestors understood better than us that information is much more likely to stick when it's part of a narrative. So the next time you have to persuade, sell, lead or teach, try finding a story: a real-life example to illustrate your point. That way, in trying to get to the point, you won't lose it.

Story telling remains an important part of managing in the middle. It's a very powerful way to communicate and get better understanding from your team of what the journey entails, and it brings excitement and enthusiasm. Remember, you need them to take each step to cross that river. The picture and understanding need to be clear.

Manager in the middle notes:

It is impossible to manage time, but you can manage your and your team's activities. Improving productivity will lead to better execution. Remember, everyone needs to be pulling in the same direction. Spend time evaluating and understanding performance. It is a good use of your time.

Everything begins with a thought, and that thought determines behavior. Be aware of the thoughts you have and the way you respond to events or situations. Improve your knowledge and understanding of your mind.

Action step: Try the 80/20 rule the next time you have a meeting with your team. Improve the productivity by having a simple agenda and set clear outcomes for the meeting.

Summary: Paint a picture by telling a story. Take your team on the journey with you and make them feel they are an important piece of the puzzle. Don't let technology manage you!

Fix the small things first, and the more difficult things become so much easier to manage.

Iain Johnston

3

How Do I "Keep In Step?"

Keeping in Step simply means keeping a rhythm. This is nothing more than applying practice and concentration until it becomes a habit. In this chapter, we will discuss a few ideas and concepts that will help you develop a rhythm and process.

Managing in the middle and being a fixer is about three things: Effectiveness, measurement, and consistency. Here it is depicted as Einstein's $E=MC^2$ formula.

$E = MC^2$

Effectiveness = Measurement X Consistency^2

It's not so much about managing your time; it's about managing activities around these three areas.

Effectiveness is a function of the results we get. Effectiveness comes from improving the way an organization, in general, and you as a manager, in particular, work. This is achieved not only through the implementation of HR best practices, policies, and procedures but also by working using **simple** and **effective** ways that generate **measurable** improvements in results.

Is it better to be effective or efficient? Efficiency is a function of the volume of work we do and doing more work in the same amount of time. We can increase our efficiency. Efficiency goes up when we implement the tools and processes available that increase speed and the outcome and result, or save time by eliminating steps that are unnecessary. It could be said that we need to be both efficient and effective, and I agree. However, for the purposes of this formula, efficiency comes from all the technology available to us, and effectiveness comes from our ability to apply the information and execute.

Measurement of the correct information will ensure we get the results we need, not want. We may want to capture information like how many customer visits a salesperson makes in a week, but unless we are going to measure their productivity (in other words their effectiveness), how useful is the number of visits that are being made? There is not much you can do with this information unless it's supported by more specific and detailed information that allows you to decide what will positively affect the result. We will talk about measurement in more detail in the next chapter.

Consistency in this formula is about doing the small things well *ALL* the time: both in the way you think (thought) and in the way you act (behavior).

We have talked about visualizations and storytelling: the visualization of your picture puzzle and seeing the missing pieces, and the visualization of your destination and the river crossing. All this is used to tell your story. In his book "The Power of the Subconscious Mind," Joseph Murphy, PhD, talks about the conscious and subconscious minds (or the subjective and objective minds). The conscious mind uses our five senses to compute thought and reason, and the subconscious mind acts on those thoughts impressed upon it by our conscious mind. It "sees" without the benefit of the natural sense of sight. The subconscious is your automatic pilot that triggers your nervous system and is responsible for your every action and behavior from breathing to driving a car and everything in between. As Ralph Waldo Emerson said, "Man is what he thinks all day long." What you impress with your conscious thoughts on your subconscious mind is expressed in the way you act, perform, and respond. I urge you to read this or similar books and expand your knowledge and understanding of the inner workings of your most valuable asset.

When doing a jigsaw puzzle, the first step you do is the frame: the picture border that defines the picture and sets the scene. If you are given a puzzle and allowed five minutes to visualize the picture on the box, when the box is taken away and you are left to build the puzzle, how do you think you will fare? Most likely, during those five minutes, you will study that picture with intensity and take in as much detail as you possibly can.

As I have already mentioned, effectiveness is the function of the result we get and improves the way you work. This covers so many things. Our management day is filled with activity, and sometimes, we don't always get things done as perfectly as we would like. Things left undone, or more particularly, things not done well, can become the origin of bad habits. So what are the things you want to do more effectively? Depending on your areas of responsibility as a manager, you may want to be more effective in revenue generation, profitability, organizational effectiveness, or in managing expenses (profitability and managing expenses may well fall under one umbrella in your business). You will be accountable for the delivery of certain results within a defined time frame.

What is the one area, task, deliverable, or function you believe needs to be improved: the one thing that you are not doing as efficiently as you would like? How do we apply the $E = MC^2$ formula?

Start with four questions that will help you define, communicate, and execute your strategy as a manager, your measurement of this strategy, and your ability to execute consistently.

1. What have I learned today?

2. What have I taught someone today?

3. What step (in the diagram below) am I on, and where is my team?

4. "Keeping in step," what do I have to do to get to the next step: that one step that takes me closer to crossing my river?

Yes, I did it!
I will do it.
I can do it.
I'll try to do it.
How do I do it?
I want to do it.
I can't do it.
I won't do it.

Which step have you reached today?

Effectiveness will come by ensuring each step is progressive and measured. It needs to be managed, and it will need your team to be consistent in the way they think and act (engagement).

Getting up the first step relates to attitude, and in particular, engagement; people that are disengaged in the workplace, in other words their needs are not being met. How many people on your team are on the first step, and why? There's a big difference between the first and second step! The second *("I can't do it")* step may be because of a lack of confidence, skill, or knowledge. These are all things you can work with as a manager. The first step, however, is more of a challenge for you. Who is on the first step, and who is on the second?

There are many examples of people who have done extraordinary things: the word *can't* is not in their vocabulary. These examples include men and woman who have climbed the highest mountains, rowed and sailed across the oceans, survived tragedy and hardships, and even disadvantaged or paraplegic people who have achieved extraordinary things.

So on days when you think your world has come to an end because you are stuck in traffic, have to deal with an irate client, or arm wrestle with an accounts department for a payment, think of these extraordinary people. Realize your problems are manageable when compared to the physical and mental challenges others have had to overcome and endure in their lives (albeit in very different scenarios and situations). The frame of reference you use when asking yourself the above four questions each day is what takes you one step closer to crossing your river.

As a manager in the middle, you need to get yourself and your team from "I can't do it" to "I want to do it." We will discuss this, along with the other steps, when we talk about managing employee engagement.

Apart from measurement and consistency, I am sure you can think of other ingredients to the $E = MC^2$ formula and other contributions or factors that improve effectiveness. But in this formula, I believe the combination of measuring and consistency, if done well, will form the foundation to effectively keep in step.

The visualization of the big picture helps clarify what your objective or destination looks like, your oasis if you will, where the water is blue, and the grass is green. The river crossing visualization is simply to see where you need to be, the possible obstacles you face, the stepping stones that will help you get to the other side, and your destination or objective by telling your story.

When faced with an obstacle, if you find yourself out of step, start asking yourself questions like: What information do I need? What is the first step? What support do I need? Who is performing on the team, and who is not? The steps we have discussed will help you ask the right questions and find the answers by rationally sifting through and removing the complexities of the influences that surround you.

On either side of measurement lies the **plan** and the **management** of that plan and is governed by the rule of consistency. Like all things in life, the plan, or what we refer to in business as strategy, begins with an idea, thought, or mental picture that is translated through discussion into a written document and, we trust, closely resembles the ideas and pictures we originally created in our minds.

I think the theme of this mental picture, this image we created, gets lost in translation when we put pen to paper, and this written word becomes the token of the way we manage. There are, of course, obvious reasons why this strategic document is developed and complied, not least of which is the supporting plan (be it sales, marketing, or operational) for the budget—the numbers! The ingredient that is missing as a manager in the middle is being able to translate this plan into pictures and a story so as to maintain consistency in the measurement and management of your execution. Before we get into measurement and management, let's look briefly at planning.

The word "strategy" originates from the Greek meaning "art of troop leader; office of general, command, generalship." It is a high level plan to achieve one or more goals under conditions of uncertainty. The uncertainty is because the plan has a future result, and the future is something we have neither influence nor control over.

Since time immemorial, man has been at war, and sadly continues to be. This perpetuates the need to plan and strategize the demise of the enemy. Like leadership, this strategic planning has evolved into politics and business. There are a number of ways to build the plan. Some prefer the SWOT methodology: strengths, weaknesses, opportunities, and threats, as a means to arrive at a plan of action. There are various derivatives of this process that have evolved. Some are more complicated and structured than others depending on the nature of the organization. Whatever process you choose, essentially they all revolve around the following questions:

- Where are you presently, and where is your business?

- What does the picture in front of you look like? Where do you want to go?

- What is the time frame you have to get there?

- What are the business opportunities, and specifically, where is the business (your products and/or services and sales) going to come from?

- How are you doing in executing your plan? How are you going to do it?

The energy levels and enthusiasm during your planning sessions are normally high. It does, however, generally only involve the senior management. Here lies the potential weak link in this section of the chain. If you have been part of a planning session, there are two things you need to consider as a manager at this stage;

1. As "the troop leader," how are you going to communicate—tell your story—to your team? Your team may not have been a part of this process, and you want to avoid the "broken telephone" communication where your interpretation of the plan gets lost during the process.

2. Remember that this communication is critical to defining the next step in the business cycle, which we will talk about in the next chapter. Concerning measurement, what do you want to measure and why? What impact will this measurement have on the execution? Will it help or hinder? A lot rests on you to get this right.

In your business, the strategic process will quite possibly be set with clear guidelines. In other words, as a manager you may have certain parameters in which to operate (commonly called red tape), levels of authority, corporate governance, policies, and procedures that are all put in place to manage the organizational structure. The larger the organization, the more processes there are likely to be.

If you are in a smaller organization, you may have a more entrepreneurial structure, which is not to say that a large organization may not have this structure. There are many examples of these types of companies around the world, but the point is, irrespective of what organizational culture you have, as managers, we need to scale this group or company strategy down to a "keep in step" management plan.

Managing in the middle is about having your own "plan" that helps you remove the complexities of the influences that surround you and allows you to keep in step. Your aim should be to develop an entrepreneurial approach and mindset to executing your plan.

Statistically, the percentage of strategies that have been done and documented only to find a permanent home in a drawer or shelf where they remain till the next strategic session is high.

Planning is a process of preparing for the future. It's a methodology that requires us to set targets and objectives that we want to achieve at some future date while, at the same time, analyze and evaluate ourselves now. We set up an action plan, but somewhere or sometime after that, if we aren't careful, we can find ourselves distracted and walking down another path, which in many cases is one we feel we have been down before and know it leads back to where we have just come from, or it leads to nowhere.

If you don't know where you want to go, it does not make any difference which road you take because they will all get you to your destination!

Today, business is driven by finance and technology. Do you remember the key business performance areas?

• Increase and improve revenue

• Increase profitability

- Improve organizational effectiveness: managing the connection between the organization, the customer, and the employees and work at **FIXING** the relationships and managing their needs and expectations

- Manage or decrease expenses

If you are in sales, as a sales manager, your key focus will be increasing revenue. As a financial manager, you will be watching margins and mark ups and managing the profitability, and if you are in IT or operations and human resources, organizational effectiveness will be your responsibility. You will also have an element of managing expenses as well.

So let's break down these components into our "keep-in-step" plan. Just because there is a company or group strategy, and irrespective of what corporate structures, policies, and procedures are in place, as a manager, you can still have your own simple one-page guide and picture for managing your team.

Let's say, for example, as a sales manager, you are primarily responsible for two things: **increasing** the revenue and **measuring** and **reporting** on sales activity. Alternatively, as a project manager, you are responsible for the completion of a project on time and within budget. Using the example of the river crossing, what does your picture look like? What's missing, and is it performance and/or productivity related? What is the first step you need to take? Remember, the shortest distance between two points is not a straight line, but the path of least resistance.

Yes, I did it!
I will do it.
I can do it.
I'll try to do it.
How do I do it?
I want to do it.
I can't do it.
I won't do it.

Which step have you reached today?

Take each of these steps and relate them to your team or an individual within the team. Then give an answer to each of the above questions. This will lead to a sense of accomplishment, and more importantly, give you momentum. You can only have one thought at a time; this process allows you to remove all the clutter. Keep asking yourself this question: "What is the one resource or action I need or can do now that will get me to the first or next step in that area of the river?" When you have identified this resource or action, implement it! Keep the tasks manageable, and if necessary, break the task down into smaller tasks.

A number of years ago, I had the pleasure of working with Tim Templeton, author of the book "The Referral of a Lifetime." He introduced me to the 1% Rule. Now if you google the 1% Rule, you will get a number of pages with variations of this rule from real estate to marketing and advertising. The 1% Rule is nothing more than simply breaking down a task, much like the law of cause and effect, where in order to achieve a desired effect, you systematically address the causes or stages necessary to arrive at the desired effect. With each of these tasks or processes, look for ways to improve each process by 1%. The 1% Rule is manageable and a good process to follow to allow you to keep in step.

In addition, by putting all your attention and focus on this one thing, in all likelihood, you will improve it by more than 1%.

When I talk to managers about their day-to-day activities, they have similar stories, and one word they use to describe obstacles is "clutter." It is not a very scientific word I admit, but aptly describes getting caught up in "the complexities of the influences that surround us."

Manager in the middle notes:

When you are faced with a problem, use the 1% Rule. Break it down into manageable pieces and focus on improving each piece by 1%.

Remember, consistency is about doing the small things very well all the time.

Action step: Show the people on your team the eight steps and ask them where they think they are, and what they think they need to do as a team to get to the next step?

Summary: When you are caught up in the day-to-day managing and feel overwhelmed by what is happening, stop and bring things back into perspective by asking yourself these questions:

- Where are you presently? Where is your business?

- What does the picture in front of you look like? Where do you want to go?

- What is the time frame you have to get there?

- What are the business opportunities, and specifically, where is the business (your products and/or services and sales) going to come from?

- How are you doing in executing your plan?

- Which step is your team on, and what can you do to get them to the next step?

Relate these questions to the steps and focus on one step at a time. Work at getting everyone on your team on the same step.

4

Measurement: How Do I Measure (because I can't execute without it)?

Measurement is a word used every day in business. The technology available today enables you to measure whatever you want and allows you to cross-reference where you are against whatever plan you have. This includes being able to evaluate critical information about your team and their ability or inability to achieve the team and business's objectives.

What is the information you *need* and *must* see every day that will let you make informed decisions about your business and let you evaluate where you are against where you intended to be?

All too often, senior management (usually IT or finance) decides to introduce a system into the company to measure, for example, sales activity. Sales are not where they should be, so a program like a customer relationship or sales-force management system is introduced.

There are four aspects of the information that are important to you as a manager: What is the information? What is it telling you? What is the source of this information? In other words, is it credible? What are you going to do with the information? Let me give you an example.

When I was starting to learn how to fly and had about three or four hours logged, I was flying with the instructor in what is called the "general flying area" or GFA, which is the area where training flights take place. Until you are qualified as a pilot and rated to fly instrument flight rule (IFR), you are required to always have the ground visible, which is called the "visual flight rule" (VFR).

It was a cloudy day, and I was still getting used to the instruments in the aircraft. In order to understand the importance of the information they were providing me, the instructor told me to increase my height and fly toward the clouds above me, which I did.

Now, when you fly into cloud cover, your world immediately becomes white, and you cannot see a thing. You have no visual frame of reference: no horizon, or mountain, or feature on the landscape to orientate yourself. Subconsciously, your immediate reaction is to stay away from the ground, so you tighten your grip on the stick and tense up. This normally results in pulling back on the controls and gaining altitude. Because you have no horizon as a reference, one hand becomes a little more dominant than the other, and it pulls down causing the left or right wing to dip.

The instructor pointed to the instruments that indicated the aircraft was climbing, and the left wing was down; however, to me it felt as if the aircraft was flying straight and level. Your first reaction is not to believe what you see, but if the aircraft continues to fly like this, the angle of the wings would be such that eventually there would not be sufficient air flow to maintain lift, and the aircraft would simply stop flying and stall.

The instruments are there to give you information: each one giving a different piece of information. Some information is relevant to your immediate situation, while other information is important but not critical at that point in time. What instruments are you using to measure what is happening in your business? What instruments do you have to measure the progress you are making in the execution of your plan? What instruments do you have to measure your team and their attitudes that could affect how they execute? What information are these instruments giving you? Like the fuel gauge in your car, when it is sitting on E, do you really want to second-guess the gauge and try to see how much you have in reserve? Flying is like managing in the middle, the information in front of you tells you everything you need to know to get you where you need to be. When your instruments are giving you information, do something about it!

For example: Your salespeople are each doing ten calls a day, yet they are not meeting your sales targets. You need to pay attention to the information and do something about it. Is the measurement of ten calls a day the correct information to be measuring? What is it telling you? Are they calling the right customers, and are these visits productive?

Here is an example of what we discussed previously. Knowing who is performing on your team and why and who is not performing and why is critical. *You want to reproduce those things that are being done right and change those things that are being done wrong.* If you don't understand and measure this, you may not be able to recover when your airplane stops flying! In other words, by the time you get to the end of the month or quarter, and you still have not achieved your sales targets, it's too late to do anything about it.

What about the sales call reports and the sales pipeline information? Knowing what sales activity is taking place and how much of that business is likely to convert to sales is critical information. It's the fuel gauge of sales management. The accuracy of this information, however, is even more critical. For example, a sales pipeline report measures what new business is being forecasted and at what stage of completion this business is currently. Pipeline reports look great and make for good reading in our budget year-to-date forecasts, but you need to scrutinize this information and understand what it means, or it's not really going to help you very much.

I am not suggesting micromanagement—quite the contrary. Nevertheless, as a manager, you will be gathering information from a wide range of people and platforms: Some good; some not so good. Some people experienced at providing this information; and some not. It is not a one size fits all when it comes to management. So whatever information you receive, check it first. Don't accept it at face value. Use the carpenter's rule, which is "measure twice and cut once." Double-check the information.

Measurement is all about having information that allows you to make decisions. Let me give you an example. An aircraft is subjected to the forces of nature: high winds, high and low pressure areas, storms, and all those climatic elements that can prevent it from flying in a straight line. With the help of an autopilot, a computer can monitor these climatic elements as well as the aircraft's systems and keep the aircraft in straight flight, while the pilot manages all the other complexities of flying an aircraft.

When the aircraft is in auto pilot mode, it is still subjected to the same weather conditions. Nothing has changed in that regard except for one thing. The minute the auto pilot senses the aircraft is moving off course, it immediately makes a correction, thereby ensuring the aircraft maintains its set course and altitude. So it works on **negative** feedback.

This is much like the performance appraisals: it is "constructive criticism in the interests of personal development." The idea is that by offering this feedback, we, like the auto pilot, acknowledge that we are off course and make the needed corrections. Human nature comes to the surface in the guise of our egos—our self-image—and depending on our level of engagement, we will either change course or defiantly turn off the auto pilot and try to pilot our course manually.

When people disengage and try to do it alone, one of two things will happen. They will either become disinterested and move into their own controlled environment and stay firmly within the strict definition of their job description, or they will leave the organization. You could find yourself in this position with your immediate manager, or it could be one of your team members. So as a manager, apply the negative feedback rule in keeping in step as a manager in the middle.

What is the information? What is it telling you? What is its source? What are you going to do with it? As with the autopilot, these four components of information are cross-referenced to the initial settings of your course, altitude, etc. It does not matter what managerial position, be it a small business entrepreneur, organization, or industry you are in. The principles of managing in the middle are the same. You will be required to change and fix a few things, and as with all change, the first ingredient is a compelling one: intent, desire, or need.

Before we get back to solid ground, let me illustrate the simple, but very important, method of managing in the middle by telling you the origin of the **2° Rule** that you can use to measure your team's progress.

One of the last flying exercises I had to do before completing my private pilot training and getting my license was to undertake a cross-country flight. I was flying from the coastal city where I lived to a small inland town, then back across to another coastal town north of my home base, and then back home.

Without the luxury of GPS technology, in order to undertake a cross-country flight, I first had to plot the course on a map. Next, I calculated the distances of each flying leg, and then noted the towns or landmarks I would be flying over in-between. During the flight, I had to record the actual time it took to get to each of these points, and then I compared them against the estimated flying times I had figured when I planned the flight. Using a Navigational Computer (remember, this was 1984), these times, together with other data, calculated my ground speed against the air speed indicated in the aircraft. The ground speed is the actual speed the plane is going and takes wind and other climatic factors into consideration.

In order to illustrate a key management principle, here is a short technical explanation on a very important instrument: the compass. When a compass is fitted onto an aircraft, it ceases to be influenced solely by the earth's magnetic field. Local magnetism from electrical wiring and iron or steel components has a disturbing effect and causes the compass to point toward compass north and not magnetic north. So without getting too technical, you have true north (the geographical north pole); magnetic north (the needle of a compass influenced solely by the earth's magnetic field and points to magnetic north); and the compass north. The difference between true north and magnetic north is known as "variation," and the difference in angle between compass north and magnetic north is called "deviation." Whew! Did you get all that? Suffice it to say that when plotting your course, you need to take these variations and deviations into account. The technical details are not important to the story, but, as you will see, the variation and deviation are!

Having completed my planning for this flight (mapped out the route, directions, headings, and estimated times), I filed my flight plan and set off. About ten to twelve minutes into the flight, the first landmark appeared, which was a cluster of aerials and masts on the top of a mountain. They were a little further off to the right than they should've been. This observation should have sounded a small warning bell because it was signaling a deviation! Not being too concerned about observing and digesting information you know is inaccurate or incorrect can be a result of inexperience or complacency, but both have a compounding effect on decision making!

I checked and noted the time at this point and was perhaps three or four minutes outside my estimated time to this point, which, again, was okay. I just adjusted and estimated my time to the next point and calculated ground speed. In business, perhaps I can draw the parallel to sales revenue as a sales manager or the progress on a project being managed by the project manager. You observe weekly reports and team activity information that indicate something may not be right; i.e., sales for the week are down from the budgeted month-to-date estimates, or you are a week behind a project delivery. Your reaction may be the same as mine. You don't seem that far off your budget, so you make a note to speak to your people, feeling confident you can make up the deficit, and you carry on the same course.

Well twenty minutes later, because I had not made any changes, I was now further off course and nowhere near where I was supposed to be. How did I manage to get off course?

When first setting your compass, there are a few things you need to take into consideration: the variations and deviations. If you don't, you could be two degrees off. A small angle of two degrees with time and distance opens out into a wider angle, and the gap between the two lines becomes significant.

Hence, the management in the middle 2° Rule.

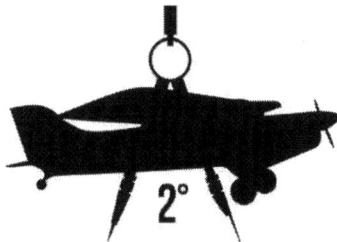

In your business, if you don't do something about the information that's telling you you're off course, the gap starts to open up between where you want to be—your business objectives—and where you actually are! By ignoring the first bit of information you received, it could trigger a sequence of events that will result in being off course.

At first, the information may seem insignificant. Don't ignore it! Check it and be confident it will not lead to further problems.

I have tried to apply the lessons I learned from my flying experiences to working with people across organizations and industries. Here are the conclusions.

1. While you don't have to use the flight-log methodology to measure each event or day-to-day activities, the importance of being able to set simple targets and "arrival" times brings an element of keeping it simple into your day-to-day management. Irrespective of what industry or organization you are in, there is always an opportunity to apply the **2° Rule.**

2. It is vital to have a measurement system in place that gives you the information you NEED to make informed business decisions. Doing something with this information will take you one step closer to the execution of your plan.

3. When you are "unsure of your position," making a decision based on information is one thing, having the right information is another, and actually doing something with this information is mandatory to managing in the middle. Observation alone will not get you where you need to be. Remembering what got you

where you are now as a manager will not necessarily get you where you need or want to be either.

4. You need at least **two points of reference for distance to come into being**. One of these reference points must be where you currently are. It's exactly the same in managing every day. You need details and understanding of the conditions in your present location. What can you see? What is the situation you find yourself in at this point? What is working? What is not? What are the missing pieces? What do you need to change, adapt, or avoid in order to get to the next point? The river-crossing example highlights this principle. The distance is marked by the points of reference, steps, or causes that bring the distance on the other side into being: into perspective.

Making a decision is something we are faced with every day. We all know the importance of making decisions, and we have our brain as the most powerful computer with which to do it. So there is no reason why we can't achieve what we set out to do, correct?

If it were that easy, life as we know it would be quite different; don't you think? What prevents us from making these decisions? What prevents us from doing it? Our circumstances are all different. We are the only ones who see the world through our own eyes, and we are unique in how we process information from what we see, hear, smell, and taste. The challenge comes when we are in an environment that is governed by the business drivers of increasing revenue, increasing profits and organizational effectiveness, and managing expenses. How do we cope?

If we think the right things and plant the right thought seeds, our subconscious minds will process these thoughts and deliver the right behaviors. But the process is sidetracked by the interference we create in this process through worry, fear, anxiety, and other destructive thoughts. We have all had our fair share of these thoughts, and as hard as we try, sometimes we just can't get the right thought process going. Our personal situations, home environment, personal relationships, financial situations, and the complexities of our own world all contribute to these influences.

As a manager, you are required to manage your team's business units or departments and lead them to increased revenue, profitability and improved organizational effectiveness, and managed expenses.

It, therefore, becomes all important for you to set aside the budgets, department objectives, your position, or job description and establish your own personally tailored plan that allows you to manage what you have to do within the parameters of your own thought processes.

So, let's get you back on solid ground where you now have a very different perspective of your management "world." Having a bird's eye view of the world lets you see the bigger picture, but as we all know, in business, our real action is right in front of us each day.

What do you measure? Well, depending on what areas of the business you are managing, you will measure revenue generation, profitability and expenses, and organizational effectiveness. All three areas of the business are detailed and complex, but you will be responsible for the delivery of some component of these. Simplistically, business is about a budget, its execution, and the people in the organization who are responsible for them.

Budgets are the foundation from which you start, but the cement that keeps the bricks together as you build the business is your ability to manage the execution and people on a day-to-day basis, which is the only truly effective thing you are able to control.

As previously mentioned, when measuring sales execution, if the only information you are measuring is the number of sales calls being made, you will tend to become so fixated with that figure that it will be all you focus on and manage accordingly: autocratically and using micromanagement. Let's look at the typical outcome. A large organization whose sales have been declining year after year chose to measure their sales-force activity using this method of tracking sales calls as their main source of information. It was an ineffective decision, and all it told them was exactly that, how many calls were made each day to customers and prospective customers! It did nothing to improve their sales.

Instead, what they should have been measuring was productivity; The reason or objective the salesperson had for going to visit these clients, and the outcomes of these visits. If you see that a high percentage of calls are resulting in no sales or no positive outcomes, as the sales manager, you can then start to investigate and understand the reasons.

Even today with all the technology available, it still boils down to knowing what you **need** to measure first, not what you **want** to measure.

The more information you have coming in, the more time you, as a manager, need to spend evaluating it. This brings us full circle to the situation where we can spend our days caught up in the complexity of managing this information and not the execution of your plan. The execution of the plan involves the people on your team.

Here is an example of the importance of knowing who is and who is not performing and why. Consider a company that implemented a sales-activity management program with their sales organization. The top-performing salespeople who had brought in the highest revenue out of the sales team were identified.

Three months after implementing the sales-activity measurement, it was found that these two top performers were only visiting slightly over fifty percent of their customers. The reasons for their sales success were that they were calling on the company's top customers who already had a strong loyalty to the brands, and the company had a very active telesales division that spoke to these customers' support staff daily: coordinating orders, actively upgrading and cross-selling, and providing a great relationship management program.

So these two salespeople were not necessarily driving the business. Of course, they had a part to play, but there were other significant influences that provided the momentum and consistency that kept these customers in the "loyal customer" bracket.

As a manager, be it sales or otherwise, knowing who is performing and why is equally as important as knowing who is not performing and why. People may be performing for very different reasons to what you perceive. Knowing what is causing the performance or non-performance lets you practice the **2° Rule**: check the measurement and change the behavior.

We have talked a lot about measurement and information. The ability to do both is actually inherent in our genes—our DNA. Let's set the scene by having a look at the people I consider to be masters of survival: the Hunter-Gatherers. Hunter-gatherers are nomadic people who lived off the land by hunting and fishing and harvesting wild food. In fact, it's true to say that all humans were at one time hunter-gatherers until the advent of farming.

All Hunter-Gatherers were masters of survival and lived in harsh and sometimes inhospitable regions of the world, and I believe their success was primarily for two reasons.

a) They had a comprehensive understanding and knowledge of the environment they lived in.

By comparison, we live in this completely different world of technology, shopping malls, and a comprehensive range of transportation from which to choose. Perhaps what we are quickly losing is the ability to use some of these basic hunter-gatherer survival techniques that are still applicable in your businesses today.

Take for example, skills using your eyes and ears: the power to observe and listen. As a manager, how good are you at listening and observing? Is there room for improvement? Of course there is! These two senses were the most important for the Hunter-Gatherers to survive. In business today, nothing has changed. Communication is one of the most popular topics in training and development programs, and at the press of a button on your keyboard, you can bring up pages of information on the subject.

So too is the ability to observe and see the big picture, while still focusing on the target or specific area without being distracted. This is a skill that requires effort and hard work.

Peripheral vision lets you see the complexities of the influences that surround you. But it does not distract you from revealing the answers that will naturally prevail through the simplicity of your own self-induced wisdom and consistently focusing on and managing the small things. Be aware of what is surrounding you, but remain focused on the task at hand.

b) ***They had a profound understanding of the animals they lived with in harmony and hunted to survive.***

What I always found interesting when reading about the Hunter-Gatherers was their profound understanding and respect for these animals. Their survival depended on their ability to hunt the animals for food and clothing, and the whole animal was used. Nothing went to waste. There was no indiscriminate killing, and often when an animal was killed, they would have a short ceremony or gesture of respect to this mighty animal that had enabled them to have food, shelter, and clothing.

The Hunter-Gatherers would observe the animals and study their behavior, interactions, moods, attitudes, and reactions to sights and sounds. This enabled them to identify when the animals displayed abnormal behavior, such as when they detected a predator, which would make them skittish, and the herd would be on edge.

I suppose deep down inside all of us, there is a little hunter-gatherer wanting to come out! Each day, I think we can release this little Hunter-Gatherer to do two things:

1. Start to understand your environment. Take time out at the start of your day and build a picture of your environment. Visualize that picture puzzle. What does it look like? Now, visualize the missing pieces.

2. Understand the behavior of the "animals" you are co-existing with and hunting: your customers, your team, and supporting management structure. Your customers are your source of food and clothing. The process of understanding their behavior is what we call customer relationship management: a piece of technology that becomes a repository of customer data and statistical information revealing trends or patterns to drive marketing and sales initiatives. What it does not allow you to do is *SEE* the customers' behavior. That is a PEOPLE thing.

If you consider for a moment that the team of people you manage is this herd of "animals" you co-exist with, how well do you understand your team and their normal patterns of behavior? Can you identify abnormal behavior? How well do you understand the individuals within the team? Who are the dominant ones; the weaker ones; the more independent ones; and what do you think causes this behavior?

I am not talking about personality profiling, assessments, and psychometric testing. I am referring to using the two "survival" senses of observing and listening.

This ability to observe and understand is an important skill to have when managing in the middle. It helps manage people at each of the eight steps.

In your career, you may have experience as a manager, or you may be new to the position, but one of the greatest attributes you can have when managing in the middle is to take the time to explore your "world." Know what it is like to walk a mile in someone's shoes as a sales representative; a driver doing the deliveries day in and day out; the warehouse staff packing and loading; or sitting in customer service dealing with customers phoning in complaints, demanding deliveries, and querying invoices. Only when you have experienced all these different jobs, do you really start to appreciate what it's like to walk someone else's mile!

We get so caught up in the cloud every day that we don't give the Hunter-Gatherer inside us the opportunity to come out and do a little observing and get a little understanding.

Steve Jobs said:

"You've got to start with the customer experience and work back toward the technology—not the other way around."

Remember, customers are not just external to your business. You have people in your internal business environment that you depend on and with whom you need to build relationships. So start with making more calls or personal visits to your team members and less e-mail, texts, and other remote control impersonal communications. This is nothing new. You have heard it all before, but repetition of these things is never a bad thing, and it reinforces that what you need to do as a manager is **"the small things well all the time."**

Because of the complexities and influences that surround us every day, you will do everything from setting budgets to attending meetings and discussions with your team and customers, constantly looking for ways to improve the business and achieving better results. These different processes require different mental skills.

I am sure you have heard of left and right brain thinking and that one side of your brain may be dominant over the other. By looking at how you approach life and problem solving, you can get an indication of which side is most likely your dominant side. I consider myself more right brain because I am more creative than analytical.

The left brain does the analytical thinking: looking at reports, managing sales activity, doing budgets and estimates, and gathering information. The right brain uses inspiration and creativity to find solutions to problems and develop action plans. The challenge is switching across from left to right brain thinking at the appropriate time, and to use the required thought process to manage whatever situation you find yourself in.

It was Einstein that said, **"Problems are seldom solved with the same degree of intelligence that created them."** As a manager, you tend to remain in the original mind-set you were in when the problem or issue arose, while at the same time trying to find a solution. What you need to do is clear your mind of the complexities and influences of the problems that surround you, in order to find the solution and fix the problem.

As a manager, try this *keep-in-step* approach. Be aware of your thought processes. Consciously try to identify moments where the circumstances require a change in your thought process. First, identify your thought patterns in your day-to-day management. When faced with a problem or decision, identify what mind-set you are in. Is it the one that you need to solve the problem? This is not an overnight solution. It's transformational development that helps us become better managers and moves us through the progressive steps from "I can't" to "I want to find the solution."

It's about changing the way you think. Get out of the clouds, separate yourself from the influences around you, and get creative. Image you are sitting on the banks of a river. You can create any picture you want. That's the beauty of our subconscious minds. The creativity and imagination you have are boundless.

So you have imagined the scene, built a picture in your mind, planned and prepared, and plotted your course. You have told your story, and now you are back on the ground where you need to execute.

Consistency—to the Power of Two

Well, what is there to say about consistency? Is it a word you are familiar with and strive to achieve? What stops you in this quest for achieving consistency? Is it because you are so caught up in managing so many things each day, constantly moving between the three sides of the triangle that we discussed in chapter one—the business, the customer, and the employee? Don't allow yourself to become overwhelmed. Successful execution is about doing the small things very well all the time. Consistency is about persistent actions and habits that get you to move through the progression of I won't, I can't, I want to, how do I do it, I will try, I can, I will, and I did it!

So you need to be consistent in three things.

Consistency in the way you think – Make a conscious effort to break free of the influences and complexities that surround you. Look at your instruments, fly out of the cloud, and see the horizon. Really observe your environment and have meaningful conversations with people to understand them and what needs drive their behavior.

Listen to people and don't play conversational mind games where you are planning and preparing your response before the other person has even finished what they are saying.

Work to perfect this art. By listening to understand, you will identify their needs, and by using the 2° Rule, you will know where they are and what you can do to help them get back on course if need be.

Consistency in the way you manage – The more you work on consistency of thought, the more you will be consistent in the way you manage. Inconsistency in the way you manage people is very disruptive. It's like playing psychological Russian roulette with people. It affects your team dynamics, and persistent, irregular management leads to disengagement. People will either withdraw or leave. Both are counterproductive to achieving your objectives and getting across the river.

Consistency in the way you measure – Know what you need and must measure. This will always be determined by what you want to achieve and what you need to understand about the details of the plan and the journey. You need to measure people's engagement, and this is done through understanding their needs. We will discuss this in the next chapter.

Perhaps I could summarize consistency this way:

You rationally need to sift through and remove the complexities of the influences that surround you. These unexpected events, and the doubts and criticisms of those around you are like strong winds that come from all directions, and as managers in the middle, there is no place to go to escape them, and you can never be sure in what direction they will strike. To change direction with each gust of wind will only throw you off course, and you will soon be exhausted from trying to fight these winds. Like good pilots, do not waste time worrying about what you cannot control. Concentrate on yourself and the skill, confidence, and determination that are needed to focus on the course of action you have set to achieve your objectives. By rationally sifting through these complexities, you will be able to reveal the answers that naturally prevail through the simplicity of your own self-induced wisdom.

Managing in the middle notes:

Do the small things very well all the time. This simple rule used every day will be a constant reminder to check where you actually are today against where you wanted or intended to be.

- Check the information you are receiving. Is it accurate, and can you make a decision based on it? Remember measurement, management, and consistency are the three links to the chain.

- You can't have two thoughts occupying your mind at the same time. Be consistent in your positive thoughts as they will reward you with positive results.

Action step: Use the 2° Rule every day to check your progress. Let everyone on your team use it to check where they are against where they should be. Are they 2° out?

Summary: Like the Hunter-Gatherers, increase your and your team's awareness by understanding the behavior and environment of all the players in the BCE triangle.

Whichever side you are on, ask yourself what is the one thing you can learn today about the players on the other two sides.

5

What Am I: Manager or Leader?

The plan is done. You have taken it and distilled it into actions, events, and activities for your team (engaged auto pilot), and now have some measurement in place to be able to give the information you need to assure you are on track and have not been blown off course. You can now manage this information and apply the 2° Rule.

Let's first have a look at the word "manager." It is a label or title that people aspire to in the business world. Every one of us wants to be recognized, and let's be honest; the title on our business card evokes a sense of success and status. The rise or step up to a manager is, of course, not as easy as writing the word manager under your name or signature. You will have your own view from your position and how you

71

interpret things like **ownership**, **responsibility**, **commitment**, and dare I say, **consistency!**

Management: what is it and from where does it originate?

Again, there are many books on management, and like leadership, a lot of management theories which I urge you to read as you develop your skills and knowledge. In this book, I have focused on the practical or hands-on approach to management: the little things that bring back the keep-it-simple approach to managing your people and business. The history of management is very interesting and gives some insight into what you see other managers doing as well as enables you to reflect and compare your own style of managing.

Management, as we understand and see its place in business today, takes us back to the start of industrialization and the factories, mining, and manufacturing facilities that employed large work forces. Along with these large work forces came the need for structure and systems to manage them and ensure they were productive, and that products were efficiently produced.

The tasks were normally quite routine and repetitive. Strong supervision was required, as in many cases during the early years, skills were being learned on the job. A gentleman named Frederick Taylor introduced the "scientific management theory." He translated this concept of specification and measurement to business tasks, particularly in these manufacturing environments. The idea was to standardize the processes as much as possible and then manage the people within these parameters—rewarding or punishing for compliance or non-compliance respectively.

In these production-line factory environments, this management theory was put into practice and seemed to work. Management was not complicated; people were placed in a structured environment with very clear rules and understanding of the consequences that came with them.

Then, in the late nineteenth century, Max Weber introduced the bureaucratic management theory, which expanded on the scientific management theory. He introduced the hierarchy structure of levels of authority and control. We can still see some of this structure in what we are familiar with today. It's interesting to note that presently, there are many companies flattening out their management structures to negate the red tape and often bureaucratic processes that stifle the link and interactive process between company and customer. This is much like we have seen in the phasing out of the "middle man" link: the agent or value added reseller, where organizations are now dealing with the customer direct.

Weber suggested detailed processes and procedures at each level of the structure. We commonly refer to these as the "standard operating procedures," "this is how we do it around here," and "do as I say, not as I do" approach to doing business. Much like the military, there were clear structures, policies, and processes down the ranks.

It was only a matter of time before the unions and governments started voicing their concerns at this rather dictatorial way of managing people and the effects it was having on the business landscape. In the thirties, the Human Resources department was born out of the clear necessity to have a department and people to oversee policies and procedure. It is a belief we still champion today. If employees are happy and motivated, it has a positive effect on the business. It is understood that your business's success, and the attainment of your objectives will ultimately be achieved through your people. Interestingly, business leaders today will agree that there is a link between engagement and business success. Unfortunately, only 25% of these leaders have a plan to address this link.

Many new theories have been presented over the years with the common thread of human behavior weaving its way through these theories and ideologies.

Henri Fayol (1841-1925) is considered the father of modern management theories. In his studies and interest in management, he had what he called the five elements: planning, organizing, instructing, coordinating and controlling. These are perhaps as relevant today as when he first identified them.

Peter Drucker followed on from these elements when he identified five categories of what he called management operations: setting objectives (which cascade down from senior to junior management); organizing; motivating; communications (which is a key skill required by any manager); measurement (the 2° Rule measuring where you are against where you need to be); and finally, development.

Beliefs in what role the management plays has also evolved over the years from believing people need to be told what to do—micromanaging them using clear rules, regulations, and procedures—to the belief that people need to be empowered; given the opportunity to use their initiative; set the guidelines and clear objectives; and then allowed the freedom to manage their activity and support through coaching, assisting, and mentoring.

As you can see, a lot of what you read and experience today is not new. The roots of management practices that define your role as a manager were first planted over a hundred years ago. They have evolved into many formats, ideas, theories and practices, all of which are now bundled into this cloud of knowledge and information that form part of the complexities of the influences that surround us. I am not suggesting this is necessarily a bad thing—quite to the contrary. It's part of our business history, but the question is, in your business environment as a manager, what has changed? Do you have remnants of these management theories which you still use? What management styles exist in your business?

Let me give you an example:

Jane (not her real name) was an intelligent and astute manager and worked in a large financial institution. She recently left the organization. Her reason? "I left because of my manager (which incidentally is statistically one of the main reasons people leave). I could no longer work in a controlled environment where her management style was autocratic, and her demands for things to be done were relentless. Her methodology was unfortunately 'my way or the highway,' and I could no longer function in this micromanaged environment." Jane had given this feedback during her 360° performance appraisal, and her manager made a notation, but nothing seemed to change.

Does this sound familiar to the management theory of Henri Fayol? In the relentless pursuit of the numbers, some managers have no other style but controlling, and are driven by ego, power, and a political business agenda.

Large organizations need to have systems, policies, controls, and measures in place because this discipline is necessary to run a business with thousands of employees. But is this the management style of today?

What was the one thing Jane could have done to manage this situation? In this type of environment, it is difficult, but she should not have been afraid to express herself. Thus, she could have met with the manager and clarified expectations, timelines, and deliverables to allow her to take responsibility for what she, as a middle manager, had been asked to do. In particular, Jane could have suggested she be given the responsibility and ownership to manage her deliverables within an agreed timeline and been left to work within these parameters rather than micromanaged in between.

Some managers, especially junior managers, may not be in a position to do this for fear of losing their job. This is what I call intellectual bullying. Subtle and even direct intimidation causes people to do one of two things—disengage or leave. Disengaging means your team members come to work and do what they have to do: no more and no less. If they are in a position where leaving is an option, they look for another job. They may even make the decision to leave without having another job lined up, as was the case with Jane. If you don't have alternative choices and need to keep your job, what can you do? It's not easy, but this example does highlight that your management style does have an impact on the people on your team and the career decisions they make.

I am sure the manager in Jane's story did not intentionally set out to manage by rule and fear every day. Perhaps she is like the scorpion in the fable about the frog and the scorpion.

One day, as a frog was sitting on a lily leaf in a pond enjoying the sun and tranquility, he was approached by a scorpion who asked him to give him a lift across the water.

The frog was skeptical and said, "But if I do, you will sting me?" The scorpion replied, "I would not do that because you would die, and I would drown."

So the frog agreed to do it. He hopped over to the side of the pond, and the scorpion climbed onto his back, and off they went. Halfway across the pond, the scorpion stung the frog, who croaked, "You said you would not sting me. Why did you do it?" The scorpion replied, "Sorry. It's just in my nature!" Hmmm, not really conducive to building relationships!

Steve Shapiro said, "The function of your business is to obtain and retain customers, and the goal of the business is to make a profit."

You need to put the relationship before your desire to make a profit. This is the challenge we face in business today as the quest for meeting the numbers often comes at the expense of building a relationship. Relationships are based on trust and are a long-term process that often conflict with the BCE organizational effectiveness triangle. The BUSINESS leaders are looking at the **business performance** and focusing on getting the numbers (the microwave approach of putting it on high, setting the timer for five minutes, and pressing the start button). Sometimes this conflicts with the CUSTOMER whose needs are for **great products, services, and value**. This also affects the EMPLOYEES who want **their needs to be met** at work. Remember, relationships are built on trust, a word that comes from the twelfth-century Norse word "traust" meaning "confidence" and treysta "to trust." Ultimately, from an Indo-European base, its meaning is "to be solid."

You have probably read about many executives in corporate organizations who have fallen from grace and been fired because of mismanagement. In many cases, they have brought the business to its knees. Perhaps they did not apply the 2° Rule and ignored the bit of information that indicated they were off course? In other words, the buck has to stop somewhere because in business, people have to take responsibility for their reckless decisions and actions, especially when there are very unfortunate consequences for those innocent people who are caught in it.

Whether you are a junior manager or have climbed the ranks with your experience and knowledge, you have to understand your position comes with a set of conditions. Much like the military, from which the concept of leadership originates, the ranks of corporal and sergeant are the equivalent of junior managers. When you are promoted from a private to a corporal and then to sergeant, you are given stripes to sew on your shirt and with them come more responsibilities. The insignia on your uniform is your business card, and when people see those stripes, their expectations are set. Military leaders in history from as early as Genghis Kahn, to the Anglo Zulu and Boer wars in South Africa, the American civil war, the Napoleonic war in Europe and the time immemorial conflicts of the middle East have engaged in the art of leadership. They developed strategy, commanded troops, and battled in raging war. Sometimes nothing was gained but a few hundred meters of territory and some piece of barren ground with the graves of the dead scattered across the landscape as a reminder of the results of the inexplicable decisions made in the name of leadership. The consequences of making a bad decision as a manager may not be as severe as this example, but a poor decision can take down a company or customers.

The question is, are you a manager or a leader? How do you see your role and what is the difference between the two? Let's call them leader/manager and a manager/leader for the purposes of identifying the role and responsibilities of these two positions. In numerous books and discussions on leadership, the topic of whether a leader is born or made has been discussed with divided agreement as to which it is: born or made? Leadership qualities are in every one of us, and there are enough examples and proof of ordinary people doing extraordinary things by showing courage, determination, and an unbelievable will to overcome hardships and extreme conditions with moments of bravery, tenacity and leadership qualities.

Of course, leadership is not always about these extraordinary achievements. It's about you as a manager, or any single one of your team, displaying leadership qualities. Each leadership book, often based on a famous person, military leader, politician, business guru or entrepreneur, brings different aspects to leadership qualities, styles, and lessons. New material resulting from either the rise or fall of a prominent person, successful business entrepreneur, or the demise of a financial institution will give rise to new leadership theories and lessons. This is the nature of the constantly evolving, sophisticated world we live in.

There are a number of examples, for instance, of financial institutions that have collapsed or have been rescued through government intervention. These institutions have been seen as "bullet proof" organizations that are the pillars of the business societies. Yet, through one weak link in the chain, one person's decision can cause the fracture in this link, and it breaks. How does this happen?

Take your position as a manager, and let's use a micro version of the scenario we just used. As a manager, you have your areas of responsibility. Generally, there are two golden rules to follow when making a decision: Don't make a decision that financially compromises your organization, and don't make a decision that legally compromises your organization.

In the case of the collapse of a financial institution, there are complex structures and financial transactions or decisions that caused the demise. This is not easily understood by the man in the street, but the collapse did not just happen. There must have been a series of events or activities that led up to this final moment. At some point, some manager, somewhere, saw information that indicated they were possibly off course (A 2° Rule moment), and perhaps when made aware of this information, said, "It's Okay. I know I seem to be a little further away from where I should be, but I can still see where we are supposed to be, so no problem. I am sure it will correct itself at my next check point." In these situations, their worlds are also filled with so much interference that some manager or leader somewhere in the system did not check his or her instruments and kept flying in the clouds.

You need to recognize that every journey begins with a first step. Every decision you make and how you react are a result of the information presented to you. How much information you have, the source of this information, and your ability to evaluate it against your own map, determine your success as a manager and leader.

Leadership lessons—what are the qualities of a Leader?

There are many aspects to leadership, and there are equally as many descriptions and words we use to describe those aspects from integrity to sincerity and everything in between. It is not my intention in this book to discuss leadership. There are many great books and authors out there that cover all aspects of leadership by those more eminently qualified through work and academic experience.

Instead, let's talk about "management leadership." Here is a working definition of management leadership—A manager, like yourself, whose role and responsibility is to manage as well as lead inside the business triangle we discussed in chapter one that is made up of the business, the customer, and the employee coupled with the following four qualities or skills that will improve your role as a manager, and particularly, your ability to manage your business in the middle.

1. Able to stay the course. You are not influenced by the complexities and influences that surround you, and you do not waste time worrying about what you cannot control, but rather concentrate on yourself and the skill, confidence, and determination needed to focus on the course of action you have set to achieve your objectives.

2. Not afraid to say what you think and feel and able to make decisions.

3. Prepared to take calculated risks.

4. Able to develop and share the big picture, tell the story, understand people's needs, and always look for new

ideas, directions, and opportunities to take the business to a higher level and be able to adapt to *CHANGE.*

This last quality ends with the most powerful word—CHANGE.

Charles Darwin once said: "It is not the strongest of the species that survives, nor the most intelligent that survives. It is the one that is most adaptable to change." As a manager, whether a junior manager or more experienced, your success will ultimately be measured by how well you have adapted both in the way you have continued to grow by focusing on your own self-development as well as your ability to develop and grow those people that work with you. Your own self-development along with those on your team, be it skills, spiritual, or knowledge, will ensure you adapt and keep pace with change.

We sometimes have a very traditional view of leadership that is born from our experiences.

We develop our heroes and people that inspire us as we go through life. True heroes, however, are those that overcame incredible hardships and unexpected curve balls that life can sometimes throw your way: people who epitomize the qualities of a management leader and command such presence and respect from the situations they are in. Everyone aspires to achieve great things. We all want to do well, and we all want moments of being the hero, the good guy, and the one others look to and perhaps want to emulate a little piece of us.

You see, leadership is not something that is confined to the CEO, the Managing Director, or even the President of the country. It's not a full-time job; it's a moment in your day when circumstances or situations arise, and you are spurred into acting and displaying leadership qualities. It's these random acts that shape you and make you a "management leader." We will see an example of this shortly when we discuss management and revisit the story of Jane, the manager who left a large organization because of the environment created by her immediate manager, and the conflict it caused with her beliefs.

Let's look at these management leader attributes.

Be prepared to stay the course:

As a manager in the middle, while in the midst of trying to fix things, you are faced with hardships, misfortunes, difficulties, danger, or just a bad day at the office. It's how you manage the situation, and the little things you can do to get through to the other side. It's how you dissect the issue or situation you are facing, and how you manage these circumstances by not immediately blaming someone else, nor doubting your own ability by blaming yourself or viewing the setback as reflecting poorly on you. Finally, you need to understand and believe that the problems facing you are limited in size and duration and can be dealt with calmly.

Not afraid to say what you think and feel:

The first thing you may think about when wanting to say what you feel is what the person or people you are saying it to will think? Will they be offended or angry? Will what you say be considered to be insubordinate, argumentative, a stupid question, or even inappropriate? In some business environments, it can be quite intimidating, especially if you are a junior manager or new to the position. As a management leader, it's important to be able to express yourself and show confidence and assertiveness without coming across as arrogant or confrontational.

Prepared to take calculated risks:

Calculated risks are exactly as the name implies. In order to take the risk, you need to do your homework. The more measurement you have to collect the RIGHT information, the more useful the information will be and will allow you to make a good decision. It's the 2° Rule. Given the information, be it visual, written, or heard, and understanding the impact of remaining on your present course, you can form a clearer picture of where you need to be and the options available to you to make a decision.

As a management leader, you are able to develop and share the big picture and tell your story. You are always looking for new ideas, directions, and opportunities for the business and to manage change.

Management leaders need to be able to move out of the complexities and the influences and apply right-brain creative thinking to be able to build the picture and tell the story. You must make a conscious effort to move into this space. We all have places or spaces where we find ourselves thinking clearer and ideas seem to flow. What prevents us from this free creative thought process is that we block this natural mental process through worry, fear, and anxiety.

Joseph Murphy in his book "The Power of your Subconscious Mind" asks the question "What do you think the master secret of the ages is, and where can you find it?" The answer, he says, is very simple. "It is the *power of your subconscious mind.* It's the last place most people look for it, and the reason so few people find it." He goes on to discuss how our minds and, literally, the power of thought work. There are many books on this subject, but this one provides worthwhile insights into how you think and how your thoughts influence your management behavior. So how do you do it? How do you deal with managing in the middle, managing the demands or expectations of the business leaders, the customers, and of course your team? The gap between theory and practice can be like trying to cross a river in a flood with fast, swirling water cascading over the rocks to form white-water rapids and strong currents tugging at the riverbanks. Along with some help and guidance from your team and peers, the best way to manage these difficult times is to "CHEW" on the situation. "CHEW" stands for:

Control: In your business environment, as a manager, there are some things you can control, and some things you cannot control. For example, you are able to control things like increasing revenue, increasing profitability, improving organizational effectiveness, and managing expenses. Managing in the middle however, cannot control factors like the weather, the state of the economy, inflation, traffic, and political unrest. In the corporate environment, things like bureaucracy and policies and procedures are part of the structure, and no amount of complaining is going to affect change.

In the case of increasing revenue, profits, and organizational effectiveness, you can most certainly control within your sphere of influence. However big or small that contribution is, it's your 1% Rule. It's the 1% that makes the difference: consistently doing the small things very well all the time!

Here is the first question to ask yourself. "Is this something I can or cannot control?" If you have no control over it, accept that it is what it is and look to find that one little thing you can do to improve the situation. There is always something you can do in the immediate circumstance or situation. You don't always see it, but with every problem, there is a solution; with every question, there is an answer.

If it is something you do have control over, something you have the ability to influence and address, then your approach is to tackle it systematically by applying a keep-in-step rule. One example that you have most likely experienced is everyday traffic! If circumstances dictate that you are on the road, and you get stuck in traffic, you simply have no control. Next time you are in that situation, look around to see the various ways people deal with it. It is what it is. Put on your favorite CD and turn up the volume.

Humility: As a manager, when you find yourself faced with a difficult situation, especially when its seems to be one you have no control over, the tendency is to express frustration, particularly when you are embroiled in a conflict situation. For example, the natural tendency may be to assert your position as manager and want to "be right" or attempt to remove all further discussion by declaring your authority and shutting down the discussion. In these moments, try to make a conscious attempt to identify your thought process and make a conscious effort to stop and change it. You may want to think of a word or person that you can use in times like this to trigger this change. I shout "RELAX!" internally to myself, and am surprised to say, I do tend to listen to myself sometimes!

Ego: This little person who sits inside your head and channels traffic through your self-image filter can be as large as life in some people and a little dormant mouse in others. This little person has probably caused more havoc in the world than any natural disaster. Ego and humility share the same office, but unfortunately, they don't often get to meet each other, and when they do, it is ego that brushes past without greeting humility in a show of domination and control.

Write the word **CHEW** in your diary or on your laptop as a reminder whenever you find Mr. Ego trying to push his way past Mr. Humility.

Worry: Well, what can be said about worry? You find yourself saying to others "Don't worry. Things will be fine." It's a well-meaning comment to try and comfort or calm someone, but as you have probably experienced, to stop worrying when you feel the very real pressures of anxiety or fear, is not an easy thing to control. Worry and anxiety induce emotion because this is your predominant thought process and you behave in direct response to this thought.

You spend most of your time thinking about the future and past, both of which you have no control. Interestingly enough, most of the thoughts you have each day are the same ones you had yesterday, and in all likelihood, will be the same as you have tomorrow. Are we creatures of habit? Our own thoughts make up so much of the influence and "noise" we so desperately need to remove each day to enable us to stay on course.

The past cannot be changed, and you have no idea of what the future will be. So what is left to do? Well, in the book "The Power of Now" by Eckhart Tolle, he talks about the past being a memory record and the future being an imagined "now." I am not suggesting you stop planning or referring to historic data or events, but if doing so creates a feeling of anxiety and worry, it will interfere with your ability to think clearly and in finding a creative solution. Consciously try to live in the NOW. To move from left to right-brain engagement, you need to change direction, and that is only possible when you disconnect from "Memory Lane" and the imagined "better situation" the future may hold for you.

Dreams and goals are what drive you to achieve, but you need to act.

Our subconscious mind does not distinguish between fact and fiction. If you think back to a conflict situation that occurred last week, for example, and you recall the discussion, you will begin to feel the same emotions you experienced at the time of the conflict. This thought about the enactment of this event is processed by your subconscious mind and immediately engages your nervous system and recreates the same emotions.

Worry is a part of our psyche. Some people seemingly go through life without a care in the world. For others, it is a constant companion. As a management leader and in order to develop the four attributes or qualities, you have to manage worry and bring it into perspective, especially when looking for new ideas and direction that require creative thinking free of the destructive instruments that retard this process.

How? Well, we will all manage it differently. You are the only one that sees your version of your world, and no one can see or feel your pain or pleasure. You can share your experience and offer advice if you have had a similar experience, but what you feel and how you process things are unique to you. How often do you catch yourself saying to someone "I know how you feel?" How do you stop worrying? Have internal discussions with yourself and be quite vocal. Talk out loud when you are alone. Say "STOP WORRYING! WHAT ARE YOU WORRYING ABOUT?" Then use the 1% Rule. Worry involves a sequence of events or factors, and one worrying thought leads to another. Break it down into pieces, and then go through the process of asking yourself this series of questions:

- What is the real issue here? What specifically are you worried about? By putting yourself in a position of having to answer your own question, it helps crystallize the real cause of your worry and anxiety.

- Is it something within or out of your control? If it is not in your control, make a conscious effort to change your thought process to something positive. If it is within your control, find a starting point in order to cross this river. Where is the first rock where you can establish your first foot hold?

- Can you do something about it? Have you got enough information? Is the source of your worry some historical event, something you said or did, or is it a concern or fear of something you think may happen tomorrow or a time frame in the future?

By the time you get to the third question, you will be in a completely different frame of mind. In your own way, you will have put it into perspective. This leads to being able to move from this analytical thinking to perhaps now adopting a more creative thinking pattern. You may find similar ways to do this and adapt the questions to suit your situation, but the process works because it aligns with the way our conscious and subconscious minds work.

The four management leader skills or attributes can be learned. As with learning to fly an airplane or drive a car, as you progress, you apply the theory, go through the steps practically, and slowly become more proficient. Confidence grows when you try something new or different and find, to your amazement, it was not as difficult as you thought it would be. It's okay to make mistakes because your development and ability to manage adversity stays with you longer than the comment or criticism made by someone else about your mistake.

These managerial leadership attributes are a small part of your daily life. They are qualities that make you a great management leader. Having the "Leader" badge does not mean that person now has a full-time job leading the troops. Most of the time, leaders, be they CEOs, politicians, religious leaders, or military generals, are involved in day-to-day managerial duties like you and only assume the position of a leader perhaps 10% of the time. Leaders are not some mystical position or status. They are you!

Managing in the middle notes:

Leadership is about those moments when people display leadership qualities: those random or occasional acts or moments that everyone is capable of doing. Don't confine leadership to the senior executives of the business, but look for it, and nurture it from your team.

Consistently focus on performance and productivity.

Action step: When you are having a tough day and things seem to be going wrong, CHEW! Don't try to control. Practice a little humility, keep your ego in check, and stop worrying.

Summary: Try to put things into perspective by asking yourself:

- What is the real issue here? What specifically are you worried about?

- Is it something within or out of your control?

- Can you do something about it?

Iain Johnston

6

Are There Some Management Principles I Can Use?

Yes. I have used eight concepts that are a combination of skill sets, attributes, and business practices to highlight those areas that will be useful for you to manage in your BCE (your business, customer, and employee) triangle, and will provide the direction to successfully achieve your objectives as a management leader. Your objectives are linked to three key business areas; namely, revenue generation, profitability, and organizational effectiveness and managing expenses.

Within organizations, both big and small, there is a need for managers to bring an element of simplicity back into their businesses. Let's have a look at these.

These concepts tie back to everything we have discussed thus far. The first illustration is the baobab tree, which depicts you—the manager in the middle! Let me explain the Baobab tree.

The Baobab tree is believed to date back possibly before the birth of Christ, making it the oldest living relic of ancient times. Doctor David Livingstone, the Scottish missionary and great explorer of Africa, described it as "that great upturned carrot," and today, it is known as the upside-down tree.

The Baobab tree is positioned as the "balance" because, in the context of management, this iconic tree in nature represents resilience, abundance, structure, and effectiveness—all of which I believe are the DNA that make up your business success.

Let's look at the eight principles.

1. The Plan—The Puzzle

The Plan — The picture puzzle is something we have covered in the book, but is one of the eight management principles because of its importance in being the foundation from which you manage. Planning is something you can do every day to help you fit pieces of your daily puzzle together. The planning stage begins with a piece of clean white paper. You start to fill it in as you begin to discuss budgets, business objectives, and all the processes you use to develop your plan. In an ideal world, it is picture perfect, but planning is always a "work in progress." Every day you need to plan an outcome.

The one thing that is often not given enough thought and consideration during this initial stage and in everyday planning is an evaluation of what resources you will need to achieve your objectives. It is important to do a gap analysis to compare what you presently have against this ideal. You will not necessarily have the perfect team and or resources, but by doing this evaluation of your resources, it gives you the basis for the development of your team going forward, and lets you budget or plan for a specific development program for your team members. This evaluation, when done every day or each week, will help you identify if someone on your team is stuck on one of the steps: be it I won't; I can't; or I don't know how to do it. It will also identify those that can say, yes, I did it! This evaluation will enable you to take the appropriate action: be it assistance, support, training, acknowledgement, or recognition.

People's skills and knowledge need to be developed in order to improve their ability to reach their potential and achieve their goals. In turn, this will help you meet the needs of the BUSINESS, on the one hand, and the expectations of the CUSTOMER on the other hand. As the manager, it is your responsibility to develop your team. By doing constant evaluations and assessments, you will see the need for any development, and believing it is what is needed, go and make it happen!

When evaluating the resources you have, particularly when looking at skills, knowledge, and talent, always begin by asking yourself, "What is the one thing I need to do that will help me and my team achieve our objective?"

2. Analytical And Observational

Analytical and observational (being curious) — **"Curiosity has a value."** This realization came about on a recent trip to Kruger National park in South Africa. As an avid, albeit, amateur photographer, I had the opportunity to do some wildlife photography.

Viewing and photographing lions, elephants, and leopards is, of course, fantastic, but so too is watching the wide variety of birds and smaller animals and creatures that make up the complex ecosystem and food chain. One such animal and a very popular resident, is the Vervet Monkey. Monkeys are intelligent and opportunists, and like all animals in the wild, their survival depends on their senses of sight, sound, and smell.

One morning, while sitting at a picnic site on the bank of a river and having a cup of coffee as I took in the tranquility and sounds of the African bush, I could see a troop of monkeys in the trees around me. Sitting quietly and watching them, I could see one of them out the corner of my eye in the tree above me. He was watching me intently, or so I thought, but what he was actually looking at was a banana that I had on the bench beside me.

He was now perhaps three feet away from me sitting in the fork of the tree, and it presented a great opportunity to take a picture of him and a close-up of those big eyes. He then jumped down from the tree, and within seconds, had covered the few feet between us, grabbed the banana, and leapt up into the tree behind me!

Thinking back to the sequence of events, this monkey employed his survival techniques of curiosity, observation, and analyzing. Using his skills in observing his surroundings and curiosity of me and what I was doing, he analyzed the information he had, sensed the opportunity when he saw the banana, and using his speed and agility, joined me for breakfast. There was a value and subsequent reward for the curiosity he displayed!

When we get caught up in day-to-day activities, we can easily lose our ability to be curious and have that enquiring mind to look for opportunity and answers to the sometimes difficult questions we get asked, or indeed, ask ourselves.

Under the pressures to survive in this busy world—be it business or personal—and being caught up in the turbulence of thought, you tend to selectively see what you want to see and hear what you want to hear. You discard what you think is irrelevant to your present state of mind and the circumstances you find yourself in. In doing so, you can miss the opportunity as a management leader to use one of the most important skill sets available to you . . . curiosity! This is a skill that can help you and your team cross the river.

3. Decision Making And Problem Solving

Decision making and problem solving — Why do we sometimes procrastinate and not make decisions? Is it because we are afraid we might exceed our limits of authority? Perhaps you are still new to your management position. You may be concerned about possible reprisal from your immediate manager as perhaps was the case of the lady with the autocratic manager, or perhaps you just don't have the information necessary to be able to confidently make that decision.

The reasons why we don't make decisions are as numerous and varied as the conditions and circumstances you find yourself in every day. However, in your day-to-day management life, you regularly face situations where you can make a decision, not necessarily big life-changing decisions, but the small ones that are the catalyst to action and activities that keep you in step. You see, not making a decision it still making a decision. You have just decided not to do anything about the matter and that the safest route is to stay where you are. This means you are not making any progress, and the other side of the river never gets any closer.

In some circumstances, it may of course be the right decision to wait. You may need to wait, BUT this will lead you to having to make another decision. What alternatives do you need to consider to keep in step and keep the momentum?

If decision making is all about deciding what direction to go and what route to take, then problem solving is about your ability to switch from a problem to a solution mind-set, remembering that Einstein said, "Problems are seldom solved with the same degree of intelligence that created them."

As a manager, also remember that you could be treated by your team as the repository of all their problems. Like the story of the young manager who walked into the managing director's office one morning and said, "Jaco, we have a problem." The managing director asked the young manager to tell him the problem. The young manager explained it to him, and the managing director replied. "First, *we* don't have a problem. *You* have the problem. And, what I would like you to do is go and discuss this problem with whomever you need to and come back to me with some ideas as to what you suggest to solve this problem. Then I will be happy to assist you in finding that solution."

When you manage in the middle, you will always have problems arising, and you will always have people on your team "handing" you the problem because they think it is your job! The lesson to remember is everyone on the team is part of the problem. It's a business problem that requires a business solution, and everyone is part of the business and team, so by default, everyone has some percentage of ownership of any problems. It could be as small as 5% or as big as 50% depending on their position, responsibilities, or degree of involvement in the cause of the problem. It does not matter. If you are part of the problem, you automatically qualify to be part of the solution.

When faced with a problem, always ask the people involved to tell you what percentage of the problem they think they are? It's an interesting question, and you will be pleasantly surprised at the response.

4. Employee Engagement And Development

Employee engagement and development — As a manager, ultimately, you are measured by your ability to create a team that performs effectively and achieves your business objectives.

A team that does not perform effectively will not be as successful, and performance and productivity will be affected, which impacts the final result. Remember, as a manager, it is not your sole responsibility to feed your team with the answers to all their questions. Remember the quote, "The teacher and the taught, together, create the teaching." It's the same as leading and being led. There is always a synergistic approach: never a one or the other.

Recognition plays a big part in engagement, and the really important things are often overlooked because they are not top of mind. Let's look at an example of this.

In schools, colleges, and universities, as in all business, people need to feel appreciated, and teachers are no different. The most important time of the year for these educational institutions is, of course, year-end when all the students graduate, and they celebrate their success as these achievements are a reflection on the standards and quality of their education. The high pass rates attained attract new students who also want to enjoy the same academic success.

What is not acknowledged, however, is that these achievements were a result of the seeds and foundation of knowledge that were planted in these pupils during their early school years. In the excitement and celebration of graduation, those teachers are now forgotten, but their impact and contribution to these graduates' academic success were considerable.

As a manager, do you ever consider what impact you can or do make in the development of new young leaders? We all aspire to leave a legacy behind to perhaps be remembered for something we said or did. You can introduce simpler formulas in your day-to-day management that complement your constant search for knowledge and understanding, and the teaching and development role that you play in your organization.

As a manager, you can't be the Alpha and Omega of knowledge and authority, but take the opportunity to share knowledge resources with your team and help them grow. People don't perceive that just because you are "the manager" you know everything; so don't try to assume that role.

Perceptions cause us to assume, and unfortunately, we begin to believe what we hear or see, and that causes us to doubt either others or ourselves.

Before making a decision based on what you have perceived, ask yourself these questions. What do I see? What do I know? What information do I have? What information seems to be missing in order to confirm or dismiss this perception?

With the underlying principle of understanding and appreciating how others think and feel as well as an understanding of the environment around you, the power of **PERCEPTION** is perhaps best illustrated by Plato, a pupil of Socrates, the Greek philosopher, and the scribe of his many thoughts and teachings. In one of Plato's more well know dialogues, *"The Republic,"* he uses a wonderful story or allegory to describe and demonstrate the world of illusions and **perceptions** that are interpreted by our senses, and through this interpretation, influence what we think and how we feel. In this dialogue, he debates how, as humans, our senses and their interpretation of information create our own "real world," and how our behavior and understanding are limited by this knowledge.

As a manager, what you see and hear and the interpretation of that information creates your management world. Your behavior and understanding as a manager are limited by this knowledge.

Plato's allegory tells of prisoners who have been chained to the floor of a deep cave for many years. Facing the back wall of the cave, they are not able to see behind them due to the method of bondage used to secure them. Over a very long time, the sounds they hear and the shadows projected on the wall before them become their world, and as Plato says, "The truth would be literally nothing but the shadows of the images." Their reality is the shadows on the wall and the sounds they hear but cannot see from where they come.

He then goes on to tell that one of the prisoners is freed. As he stands and turns to walk toward the light at the opening of the cave, he suffers pain from the glare and is unable to see the realities of this new environment. It will take some time for him to change his perception of this new vision and understand the limitations he had from his cave experiences. He will have to become accustomed to the sight of this new world, and he will by casting his eyes on this new experience and comparing what he is seeing to his "own world" experience from the cave.

In experiencing this new world, Plato suggests that when returning to the darkness of the cave, he will experience poor eyesight, having lost the acclimatization of seeing in the dark. This will make him appear ridiculous to those prisoners who still remain. In addition, can you imagine the conversation he has with the remaining prisoners in trying to explain this "new world" he has just experienced? It is at this time of uncertainty that we pass judgement, or when faced with a challenge within our world, that we are likely to err as our judgements are often affected by our own blurred "vision" and perception as we compare what we see to what others tell us they see!

This story illustrates the ease at which we make judgements and draw conclusions about circumstances, people, and our own behavior. As a manager in the middle, allow yourself time to adjust to changing situations before making a judgement call. Try to understand and appreciate that sometimes people on your team need to acclimatize to the situation they find themselves in. Driven primarily by fear, people do not readily accept change, and as such, attempt to stay within the shadows—their comfort zone—believing this to be the safest place to be . . . in their world!

Perceptions grow from not taking the time to listen. Sometimes you get into the zone of being "the boss," and you tell others "do as I say, not do as I do." By doing this, you miss important signs. And so begins a spiral effect that can ultimately lead to disengagement.

One keep-in-step concept is the "ride with" program, which is simply going out with sales people (or any member of your team for that matter) to visit customers. This is something that, as a manager, you need to do more often. These "ride with" activities, when done correctly, transform the car into a mobile classroom, and the drive around to visit customers becomes a relaxed environment to communicate.

These "ride with" programs are nothing new. They have been and still are taught in sales management courses. They are still one of the most simple and fundamental activities a manager can do, and you can use it to become a better management leader.

In a completely fresh environment, you get to observe and listen; ask questions to clarify perceptions or assumptions; analyze and gather information (measurement); and then enter a meaningful and constructive dialogue.

The concept of riding with someone does not necessarily have to be driving around visiting customers; it could be as simple as getting out of your business environment and meeting in a coffee shop. It's all about finding a pace that changes you and your team's mind-set.

You see, it's at times like this that you identify peoples real needs, and particularly, skill and knowledge development areas. People are like onions. They have a number of layers. On an onion, when you peel away the outer protection layer of dry brown skin, you will expose a white and juicy interior that is much more appealing. People also have natural protective layers. It is their camouflage to prevent people from seeing or understanding their true feelings. Our built in hunter-gatherer protection modes mean that what you see on the outside is not necessarily what is on the inside. People sometimes suppress their feelings and remain guarded about their comments and opinions. All this makes your job as a manager that much harder.

Remember, you have a task to do. You have a river to cross, and you and your team need certain talents, skills, and knowledge in order to get to the other side. So it is in your best interest, not that of the Human Resources department, that you ensure you have what you need. You cannot complain that the team members you have are not good enough, or people are not doing what they should be doing. You need to fix it.

Let's now look at the next four principles depicted by icons that, for me, represent the foundation of effective management. There are so many skills and knowledge blocks that it could be a book on its own. But as a manager, not paying attention to these four, in particular, can cause you unnecessary problems and heartache.

5. *Market Intelligence*

Effective market intelligence — I have spoken throughout the book about information and the importance of being in a position where you can make a decision as to which way to go, what direction to take, and which offers you the least line of resistance. The shortest route between two points when crossing the river is not necessarily in a straight line. It's the line that offers the least resistance and gets you around the areas of rapid and deeper water.

Now, market intelligence does not mean you have to re-enact the life of James Bond or go to spy school to learn the tricks of counter-espionage and perhaps throw in a quick course in self-defense. It's about gathering information that can be anything from competitor analysis to market place and industry research for a new product or service you wish to launch. Like the Hunter-Gatherers, its understanding the environment and behaviors of the "animals" you hunt and live with, and it is all considered "market" intelligence.

Gathering information has and always will be a necessary part of what you do. It began with the Hunter-Gatherers, then through the ages of wars, the industrial revolution, and now to the business world as we know and experience it today. The Hunter-Gatherers needed to gather information in order to survive. Their tools were rudimentary, and therefore, necessitated the use of skill, their senses, and through observation, taking in pieces of information that started to form a picture. Your survival as a manager in the middle is also dependent on your ability to gather intelligence.

Covertness and a profound understanding of their environment allowed them to track animals. When following the animals where the trail or paw prints were not very clear, such as over rocky ground, the Hunter-Gatherers had to gather information to help them deduce which direction the animals were heading. Simply to walk along a path or trundle through the undergrowth in the hopes they would be lucky and chance on some animals would have inevitably resulted in them going hungry!

What is your present market intelligence like? What do you need to know and understand, and more importantly, what skills does your team already possess? Do they simply follow the path hoping they will come across what they need to know, or do they systematically go about finding the correct information?

We have the ability to store so much information today; your smart phone has more technology in it than the Apollo11 Space craft! If they could get to the moon with their technology, you can certainly get to your destination with the right information. Get rid of the clutter by understanding what information you need, what measurement you will use, and what you need to do to get this information on time.

6. *Communication And Managing Expectations*

Effective communication and managing expectations — The word "communication" is perhaps one of the most commonly uttered words in the corridors of organizations today. In the global village we call home, it's no longer just about communication in our office environment; it now expands from America to China and everywhere in between. From e-mail, Skype, and sms to webinars, we talk to the world.

There was once a world without all this technology, albeit a little slower than today's, but a world where the principal communication was talking. The need to speak to people beyond our own little world, however, sparked the revolution that introduced the telephone: the beginning of quick and easy global communication.

In order to understand what holds the "managing in the middle" wheel of communication together, we need to travel back in time to around **1665** to be reminded of Newton's universal law of gravity: a law that was created from Newton's observation of an apple falling from a tree. The universal law of gravity explains that every single person or object exerts a gravitational pull or force on everything around us. As strong or weak as this gravitational force may be, it varies according to the mass of the objects and the distance between them. If, however, you double the distance between the objects, the attraction or force becomes four times weaker.

In drawing an analogy to your business, the closer the business, its employees, and its customers are to each other, the stronger the gravitational pull. In other words, the closer the people who make up the BCE triangle are to each other, the stronger the business engagement. Which means the BUSINESS, the CUSTOMERS, and the EMPLOYEES have a better opportunity to mutually satisfy their needs! You cannot and will not develop strong relationships and build trust that is essential to keeping your wheel turning by technology and remote control alone!

The key to managing in the middle is being able to develop and share the big picture, tell the story, understand people's needs, look for new ideas, directions, and opportunities for the business, and adapt to **CHANGE.**

As a manager in the middle, you are this invaluable link between the three sides of the triangle and the one to manage their expectations.

Managing expectations is one of the biggest challenges that management faces in the workplace today. I sometimes think managing the complexities of personalities requires an MBA in people psychology, and as a manager, you enter the ranks into the new world of management, often learning and leading as you go and finding yourself woefully unprepared and sometimes, perhaps a little intimidated.

Is there light at the end of this tunnel? How do you keep in step? Well, start every day by asking yourself the question "Who do I need to communicate with today?" You may have any number of people you have to talk to every day, but is there one person who you can communicate - not just talk to - who will assist you in achieving your objectives?

Is there one person you can communicate with today that will make a considerable difference to his or her day? By talking to that person, you will not only get to understand something a little better, but more importantly, through this discussion, you can manage your and his or her expectations! Keeping in step is about doing the small things very well all the time. It's about putting your left foot out first, followed by your right, and the consistent steps that take you to where you need to be.

It does not matter what chaos or influences you are surrounded by. You can choose the keep-in-step activities, the little things that do make a difference, not only in the way you manage, but in the people's lives that you lead. We will talk about engagement in the next chapter.

Keep-in-step moment — Talk to the people. We live in a world that is more turbulent than ever before. On the one hand, the world is a global village, and yet it is disconnected in so many other ways. People are tired of not being heard. We have seen sweeping unrest around the world where violent confrontation has led to governments being toppled and changes being made from Egypt to Crimea. This change has unfortunately created uncertainty and tentative new regimes trying to restore the balance. This may take time, but the point is, irrespective of the outcomes, they have arisen out of this need for people to express themselves, and sadly, sometimes pay the price for this opinion.

Communication is in danger of becoming a tool to meet the numbers. You say the right things to customers or the people on your team and in your organization in order to close the deal or meet your particular objectives. Then you get back on the treadmill, pushing hard and wiping your brow, while cranking up the elevation in training for the next hill that is sure to be around the corner. Technology will help you keep in touch with the people: send an e-mail, send customers a birthday wish, check the sales pipeline, and arrange another meeting to press home the urgency of the need to chase the numbers and drive the team to set more objectives and time lines. Whew! This is hard work, and the frustration you feel is from people being disengaged, not motivated, and frustrated!

This picture may not represent your business environment, but perhaps there are a few things that strike a chord? In some organizations, this picture is not at all dissimilar.

In your organization, what does it look like? Is there room for improvement? This week, make a commitment to talk to someone. It does not matter who: a work colleague, one of your team, or even senior management and see if you can learn something. I am not suggesting you search for their deep-down secrets, but see if by talking to them, you are able to get a glimpse of the world from their perspective. It will give you valuable insight as to how other people think, which may be quite different from the way you think and drive your behavior. It's a simple exercise ... or is it? Ask the questions.

- What have I learned today?
- What have I taught someone today?
- Which step am I on, and where is my team?

Keeping in step; what do I have to do to get to the next step; that one step that gets me closer to crossing my river?

7. Confidence and Assertiveness

"Nothing has changed except my attitude – so everything has changed."

Confidence and assertiveness; you need to believe in yourself and your own ability. Managing people is the biggest challenge you are faced with when managing in the middle, you are managing your relationships with senior managers above you, as well as energizing and mobilizing the people on the teams below you in the quest to meet the numbers. What drives your success is ultimately your attitude; sometimes a change in attitude changes everything.

Your ability to manage people around productivity, performance, and engagement requires the feeling of assurance or self-assurance. You become a little less assured when you are perhaps working in your areas of weakness. For example, some people are very structured, organized, and very efficient when it comes to administration and writing reports. Some people are less structured or organized. For these people, they have to find other ways to deal with this ever-demanding requirement in today's business world. You need to work to your strengths and get the right assistance to manage your areas of weakness—those things you don't do that well. I would recommend reading Marcus Buckingham and Donald O Clifton's book "Now Discover Your Strengths."

Having these areas of weakness are not a design fault. They are just areas that are not as developed as the areas of strength. You are who you are. Marcus Buckingham clearly illustrates the importance of working to your strengths and managing your weaknesses. You clearly need to know the areas in which your talents lie, and together, with your accumulated skills and knowledge, focus on where you know you can make a difference. As for those dreaded weaknesses, "subcontract" out to people that have them as strengths.

What are your strengths and weaknesses? What do you do particularly well, and what are those "not always talked about" areas you don't do well and contribute to you not being as confident as you need to be when managing people?

Ask yourself these questions each day: What have I learned today, and what have I taught someone today?

8. *Accountability*

Accountability — As a manager, you need to be accountable and take responsibility for your own deeds and actions, as well as being held accountable to someone (senior management or an individual or your team) for your actions or deliverables.

As a manager, you need to manage adversity. That means not playing the blame game. Ignorance of the law is not an excuse to do something illegal. You can't say you did not know the law or the rules. The responsibility is always on you to employ common sense, and if in doubt, find out. It is presumed that there is enough access to information and resources available to interpret what is wrong and what is right.

As a manager, you expect people to do what is expected of them and get things done. You expect a person's CV detailing academic qualifications, skills, knowledge, and achievements to amply illustrate they have the qualifications to do the job.

When interviewing for a position, people need to be able to translate this CV into a clear and cohesive presentation that together with their qualifications and talents meets or exceeds the expectations of the deliverables this position requires and demands. In other words, "it does what is says on the box."

As a manager, you will also have a job description or positional contract that details your role and responsibilities. When you do your performance reviews, in whatever shape or form they might be, this is where you take ownership and responsibility for the performance and results for which you are being reviewed.

Irrespective of the market or environmental conditions, competitor activities, the economy and extenuating circumstances, or influences involving people, the buck has to stop somewhere, and it's usually at your desk!

So in keeping in step, what are the small things you can do as a manager to improve accountability and hold your team accountable for what they do?

You need to hand over the responsibility of the little things. For example, in the sales environment, have a discussion with the salesperson and take three particular customers: one you would consider a loyal customer, one that is doing okay, and the third that is either doing badly, is a new customer, or a prospective customer.

Given the fact the function of your business is to obtain and retain customers, ask the salesperson to give you one thing they will do with each of these three customers that will result in either obtaining or retaining their business, and then hold the salesperson accountable. What do they believe the consequence for not achieving these objectives should be? How do you increase revenue? One customer at a time!

This example could apply to any situation where you have expectations for someone to accomplish something. You see, if you are not clear about your expectations of accountability for each person, it will have a domino effect on you when the accumulated and collective results of the people you manage are presented in your month-end or quarterly report: a time when little else counts but the numbers!

The 2° Rule applies as much to accountability as it does to direction. Keeping in step allows you to guide, direct, and measure. It's the way you communicate and with whom. Whether it's telling, selling, coaching, or mentoring, you adapt what you say to the appropriate audience and what you are addressing them about.

Accountability — You must take into account facts, assumptions, suggestions, as well as present and forecasted scenarios. All are a part of the jigsaw puzzle you have to build. Management is fun; it can be exciting and even frustrating, but it's also very rewarding. As you fit each piece of your puzzle into the picture, remember: manage, don't control; inject a little humility; reject a little ego; and worry less by keeping in step and doing the small things very well all the time.

From strategy, measurement, and management, we have set the formula $E = MC^2$, which led us to the management leader formula of the eight icons. Remember, as a management leader, it's the **needs** of your people that drive their behavior, not necessarily your leadership influence. We all have needs; sometimes people have difficulty articulating what their needs are. I am not talking about the basic needs for food, water, and shelter, but the more deep-seated needs that influence their engagement in the workspace. What is the impact on your team members' needs, on your business in general, and you in particular?

Managing in the middle notes:

As the manager in the middle, you are like the Baobab tree. You are the balance between the BUSINESS, the CUSTOMERS, and the PEOPLE. This iconic tree represents resilience, abundance, structure, and effectiveness. Remember that perceptions lead to quick judgement and spontaneous decisions. Use the carpenter's rule of measuring twice and cutting once. Before you make a decision, check the information or ask for clarity.

Action step: At the end of every day, if you can give at least one answer to each of these questions, then you have made a small but significant impact in the lives of two people! What have I LEARNED today? What have I TAUGHT someone today?

Not all eight principles we discussed in this chapter may be applicable or appropriate to you at the moment, but select one that you would like to improve and apply the 1% rule.

7

Needs? What's This Magic Ingredient?

Let's start by looking at the foundation of needs using Maslow's hierarchy of needs model in which he identifies what he called the basic needs of humanity.

Physiological needs: These physiological needs are our basic survival requirements and essential for us to function. As a result, these needs (air, food, drink, shelter, warmth, and sleep) are the most dominant and important of all. Many of us take these needs for granted every day, yet there are still millions of people around the world who are denied these very basic physiological needs. Let's look at an example.

In an informal settlement in South Africa, there is a community of volunteer teachers headed by a lady called

Margaret Xaba. They look after orphaned children, provide after-school care, and assist these children in their school and home work. They also provide support to the grandmothers of these children who shelter, clothe, and feed them. This small group of teachers and social workers also provide basic primary health and educational awareness to the community at large on personal hygiene and diseases like HIV, Aids, and other sexually transmitted diseases.

In a discussion with these teachers on needs and what they felt motivated them, and people in general, one of the volunteer workers said her need was to have "shelter." When asked what she meant and in what context, she replied that she lived in a small shack made of a mixture of metal sheets and boards, stones, and other support materials. She does not have a standard brick or similar structured house, and here she is spending every day taking care of other people who, quite frankly, are in the same situation as her, yet she can put her needs aside and focus on the needs of others. This is quite remarkable given the fact her own basic need is not being met. Selfless acts are at the very core of human kindness. What are the basic needs of your team?

Let's look at the next tiers of Maslow's human needs.

Safety: With food, water, and air taken care of, the next need is that of safety, which apart from the safety of feeling secure and safe from physical danger, includes unsafe work environments that may put people's physical safety at risk as well as the psychological safety of the workplace that may affect emotions, motivation, and sense of security.

Social: The next need is love and a sense of belonging in both personal and business environments: the need to feel a part of a family, group, or tribe. In the business environment, this can be met through teamwork when your team gets together and works toward a common goal.

Esteem: This is achievement, status, success, dominance (like Alpha female Hyena or male Lion), prestige, and respect (both for self and from others). Pride is what drives us in our quest to reach for the top of our careers, academic achievements, sporting career, the top of the mountain, or even run a marathon. In becoming a manager, this signals your status that can lead to gaining other people's respect, but if you are not confident, you may not necessarily have self-respect, and as a result, overcompensate by asserting your dominance. The same applies to the esteem of your team. What issues need your attention? Is the lack of self-esteem the reason why some of the people are disengaged? If they are, what is causing it? Some people may have higher degrees of ambition and drive than others; however, everyone desires recognition and acknowledgement that, to them, signifies success or achievement.

Self-Actualization: This need is met when we reach a stage of independence in our lives that allows us to achieve our full potential and be the best we can be. It is a sense of self-fulfillment and gives a sense of purpose in our lives.

Maslow believed we could all attain self-actualization. The reason we don't or have not achieved it yet is because this life's journey, this steady climb to the realization of our potential and fulfillment, is blocked by our failure to meet a lower-level need. In the work environment, it could be a job loss on the one extreme, and on the other extreme, it could be a dominant or autocratic manager as Jane experienced.

Today, the principles of Maslow's theory has been expanded and massaged into a number of different programs and systems that are the cornerstone of human and organizational development. From psychometric testing to employee surveys, we are constantly testing, probing, and trying to measure the temperature of the organization to discover what people think and feel. How do we get people to live our vision and mission and display our values? By doing psychometric testing, we employ the "survival of the fittest" principles of nature to ensure we get the best and strongest recruits in our business.

But ultimately, it is the needs of these people, irrespective of what position they have in the business, in general, or on your team, in particular, that drive their behavior. If the behavior of any member of your team is not the behavior required to get you to your destination, your job becomes that much harder.

Efficiency, effectiveness, and productivity can all be pieces of the puzzle that are missing, so your picture will be incomplete.

Let's look at how we change behavior. Here is a quote from Jack Welch, the ex CEO of General Electric, who said "Any company trying to compete ... must figure out a way to engage the minds of every employee."

One of the major causes of inefficiency in a business today comes from working relationships. How much time are you spending on trying to manage people, their issues, and finding ways to bring everyone in line, so you can keep everyone on track to reach your destination?

Employee surveys are done around the world and are very useful in gathering information. This information helps leaders and managers understand the "climate" and becomes the catalyst for them to introduce initiatives, development programs, and even incentive schemes that dangle the carrot, in an attempt to reward people for doing what, in a sense, they were employed to do, and what their CV said they were qualified to do.

With surveys, the information is gathered and analyzed by management who then evaluates it and takes on the responsibility to do the repair. It is management that initiates the surveys and the interventions to address the issues and challenges that have evolved from the survey. Each intervention is often seen as another management agenda.

Organizations continue to do surveys, continue to introduce programs to deal with disengagement, and continue to apply this downward pressure to try to affect change. While organizations need to understand the business climate, the real responsibility to understand the people rests with you, the manager in the middle. You are in a unique position to succinctly evaluate and understand the real needs of your team as a micro environment, and then take responsibility as a team to address issues and challenges and fix them.

Some organizations now resort to running a survey every two years in an attempt to remove the stigma that is unfortunately attached to them. The question is how do you manage engagement between these surveys?

Remember the history of management theories? There are some companies today that still have not changed the fundamental way they manage people. We have all heard the saying "our people are our most important asset." Like the Baobab tree, they are the roots of your business. They are spread throughout your business and provide the foundation, strength, and nutrients on which the business grows. So why do we acknowledge they are the most important assets and then strive to test their strength, resilience, and moral fiber through a survey that, with some exceptions, gives us information that, quite frankly, we already know, and ask questions about the organizations needs and not those of the employee?

Managing in the middle means you are the greatest source of information and the most important link between the EMPLOYEE (your people), the CUSTOMER, and the BUSINESS (the leaders). There is no doubt that your position as a management leader determines the speed and success your business has in not only meeting the numbers, but more importantly, the improvement of employee engagement through productivity, efficiency, and effectiveness.

If you believe your people are your best asset, then what you have to do is understand their needs. As we have seen with Maslow's theory, as human beings, we are driven by these needs. Understanding these needs as a manager is where the secret lies. When it comes to understanding needs, I think the employee surveys fall a little short. You can't keep pushing down all the time and constantly trying to draw information out of people who have become inherently distrustful of these surveys, skeptical of the management's intent, and more importantly, see little change and response to their environments and input.

So what are the things we need to measure, learn, and understand before we can assume our management role and teach, guide, and coach? And yes; there will be times when we need to manage those difficult things that are invariably part of business, with a little more control and assertiveness.

Pain points such as motivation and conflict are the unfortunate result of people coming together. This melting pot of personalities, egos, needs, and expectations will inevitably result in differences of opinion and sometimes, because of our intolerance of others and poor communication skills, conflict arises. As a manager, you can make the mistake of assuming people are like you—that they have similar needs, values, and therefore, would like to be treated as you would. Well, the reality is that people are dramatically different. What motivates you to get out of bed (and make it) will be very different to another. What motivates you may be the very thing that demotivates another.

There are as many factors that affect employee engagement as there are programs and interventions to address them. McConnon International for example has a program called "An Even Better Place to Work™" which uses seven indicators for measuring and managing employee engagement. These are feeling valued, motivation, managing differences, ownership, conflict, being open, and feedback.

These are all common employee engagement factors that we find in our business today. They are nothing new, and you have experienced them (or will) at some stage or another: either as a manager having to deal with these issues or within your own personal space. Looking back at Maslow, we can see where things like motivation, feeling valued, and ownership fit into his theories. What is interesting about this program, however, is the process they use to hand responsibility to the team leaders and individuals within these teams for the measurement, management, and improvement of their seven employee engagement areas.

The journey from the first and fundamental stage of physiological needs to the point of self-actualization is not a journey you take alone, and you are subjected to any number of influences and assistance from people around you in every stage of your lives; however, you are the only thinker in your world, and you make the final decision in your own mind as to what you accept and what you don't.

Things like motivating others can become extremely difficult to manage or manipulate. As managers, you can influence the business environment in which you want your team to operate, but you need to hand over the responsibility for change to the individual people and the team at large.

Let me give you an example. A few years ago, I was out one Sunday morning riding my bicycle. In a moment of lapse in concentration, as I went around a corner, the front wheel slid from underneath me, and I fell onto the road, landing with my hip on the curb. The net result was I cracked my femur and had to have three pins inserted in the bone. I was then sent home, and for the next six weeks, a pair of crutches was my constant companion.

The Orthopedic surgeon who did the operation was responsible for stabilizing the fracture and setting the leg, but then handed the responsibility for the repair over the next six weeks to me: my body provided the chemistry to heal the bone. Six weeks later, with the assistance of some physiotherapy and exercise, I made a full recovery.

The same repair process applies in the workplace. You and your organization are responsible for setting the scene and creating the environment that will facilitate and support the repair. However, the individuals, in their team environment (with you), must take over the responsibility for the repair.

As a manager, you are part of this repair process. You are an integral part of the team. The discussion you have with them should be about how WE are doing around OUR employee engagement indexes; inviting feedback on what everyone thinks may be the contributing factor to these scores; and what WE are going to do to improve them.

The crucial words here are WE and OUR. Too often as a manager, we have a "them and us" approach to the way we manage our people. Having a "We" and "Our" approach is not a sign of weakness or softening of our management stance—quite the contrary. There are times when we need to be assertive and make difficult decisions.

When you hand the engagement responsibility over to the people, two things happen. First, people generally will respond and feel it positively impacts their self-esteem, and secondly, people begin to show leadership qualities. It's about transformation. If you want to change the culture, you need to do so from the individuals upward. They determine the pace of transformation, not the powers that be. You can't put employee engagement into the microwave, turn it to high, set the timer for ten minutes, and press the start button. You can't chase the numbers, and leave the people behind!

Leadership, as we have discussed, is not all about the CEO leading the company astride his white horse, directing the troops, and pouring over strategic maps and battle plans. Leading the business and leading the people are different. Your role is to manage and lead the people. What better way to manage than having your team help you by making their own leadership decisions and taking responsibility for the repair. Quite frankly, you can't do it for them! Remember, the teacher and the taught, together, provide the teaching - the leader and the led—you and your team.

Managing in the middle notes:

The key to managing in the middle is not to assume that people are like you and have similar needs and would like to be treated like you. **They are very different and are motivated by their own self-interest, not yours.** People's needs drive their behavior, not necessarily your managerial influence.

Their needs will determine which step they are on and whether they will climb the next one. Understand and address these needs, and they will climb the steps with you.

Summary: Focusing on understanding the needs of the EMPLOYEES and working with them as a team in giving them the responsibility for the repair will result in more engaged employees. Engaged employees are motivated, take ownership, and positively embrace building relationships with the CUSTOMERS. This means the customers have their needs met, so they become long-term purchasers of your organization's products and services, and that satisfies the needs of the BUSINESS leaders. This combination creates better business performance.

Action step: Ask your team what is important to them: things like motivation, feeling valued and ownership. Start to build a framework with them for these needs and then have the discussion about what to do to address them. Develop the understanding that as a team, they, including you, are responsible for the repairs.

8

Shall We Wrap It Up?

We live in an ever-changing world; children born today will never know a world without technology. What we once thought of as only concepts have become a reality. Electric and driverless cars are in existence and no longer confined to the world of science fiction or the imagination of car manufacturers. Here is an example of life in the fast lane: a taxi ride through the streets of New York. New Yorkers do it every day. They take a journey in the famous yellow cab. It's a symbol of New York and immediately recognizable from the movies. The taxis traverse the city without seeming to bash into each other like bumper cars. How do they manage to avoid each other?

It appears that the unwritten rule, or common understanding, is that they simply focus on the road in front of them, and the cabs behind do the same. From the perspective of a visitor, this seems to be organized chaos, but to the driver, it makes some kind of sense. Through this common understanding and "cabby rule," the system appears to work. While there may be an occasional bumper bashing, for even their world is not perfect, it is not something you see often.

This concept of only focusing on what is in front of you is an interesting one. If you are continually looking in your rear-view mirror, the likelihood of you bumping into something is quite high. Your rear-view mirror, the view you have of your past and your history of business and personal experiences, can affect you in two distinct ways as a manager. One is to see how far you have come and what you have achieved. This is a good thing. The other is the human instinct of reliving events or circumstances of mistakes and business experiences that immediately conjure up the same emotions as when these historical events occurred. This is a bad thing, and if not careful, you could spend too much time in these negative emotions.

As the saying goes, "We learn or should learn from our mistakes." In "The Decision Book" by Mikael Krogerus and Roman Tshappeler, they talk about the types of mistakes people make, the various levels of mistakes, and the different factors that contribute to the mistakes. What will help you understand how to prevent a similar mistake is knowing whether the mistake was due to you having the wrong systems and processes in place, or because these systems were carried out incorrectly? Are the mistakes happening because of a lack of skills, knowledge, or disengagement on the part of one or a number of your team that is resulting in disinterest and complacency? The next time you or your team makes a mistake, check for the reason why. What was the system, process, or people issue that caused it? The answers will help you find the solution.

Managing in the middle means you have a steady stream of information coming from the BCE triangle that we discussed in the first chapter: the business, the customer and the people all demanding attention and wanting their needs met. All this information comes at you fast and furious, and before long, you feel you are on the hamster wheel again. Let technology assist in becoming more efficient. Don't let technology control you. It is the people on your team that will help you be more effective.

The repair work needs to be done by the people. Your job is to set the scene and create the environment that allows them to do it. Your corporate policies, corporate governance, and political red tape are not an excuse. However, they can be irritating factors and become an obstacle when you are standing on the bank of the river and all you see is red tape and company policies in the form of frothing water flowing over the rapids that will surely sweep you down river if you get caught in them.

Become a story teller. Look back to your childhood and remember the stories you were read or the stories you read to your young children. Relive those moments; we all have memories of when we had stories read to us. We let the stories capture our imagination and create our own pictures. Be a good story teller. Share your thoughts and create the environment for the people to take responsibility for managing their own development.

Draw your own map. At some point, you have probably sat next to the window in an airplane and had a bird's eye view of the countryside, mountains, rivers, and the open undulating landscape. Let people gather around and look at it. Show them where they are going, what lies in-between, and the distances from each check point. What is the course you need to set, what are the times you believe you will take, and what measurement is in place to check the progress—your own and the team's?

What will complicate this process? The more people involved, the greater the risk of a communication breakdown. Technology will improve your efficiency, and the people will improve your effectiveness. Both are important, but effectiveness is how well you do all the things that are necessary to get the money in the bank.

Take the four attributes of a management leader, and together with the questions you need to ask yourself each day, develop your own style of managing in the middle that is free from the complexity of the influences that surround you. Captain your boat with skill and your own self-induced wisdom.

You have the tools, the picture, the flight, and the river crossing to do it. Look back for a measure of your journey and the successes of each step.

"We must not cease from exploration, and at the end of all our exploration will be to arrive where we began and to know the place for the first time." TS Elliot

In his book "The Power of Now," Eckhart Tolle emphasizes the importance of being what he calls "in the now," and not being what he suggests as a slave to our minds. The mind is a very powerful tool. However, as with any tool, you must use it correctly, and then when you are finished put it aside. In other words, find the time to stop thinking.

What he suggests is changing the way you think to be more in the "now" . . . more in the present moment because, as he states, "now" is the only thing you have. Your mind and your thoughts spend most of the time either in the future or the past. Both will cause anxiety and stress because we will either worry about what may happen tomorrow or about things we did yesterday. We have no control over either situation. Yesterday has gone, and tomorrow has not yet arrived. It takes practice and conscious thought to constantly bring you back into the present and manage what is happening now.

Managing in the middle can be a busy place. Being a management leader is not a position with a title. It does not matter how big or small the company is where you work. The principles are the same. As a business, you want to obtain and retain customers. In order to do that successfully, you want to build the picture, get a bird's eye view of the journey and the destination, and then from the ground, look at your river and get a perspective of the obstacles and the stepping stones that are available to you.

You doing the small things very well all the time make each next step you take easier. This brings consistency, and that will keep you in step.

You are a facilitator of change. You are a *Fixer*. In the history of business, there have been trends and adaptations of a number of management theories: all of them centered on the theory of how to manage people across the finishing line.

In all my discussions with managers across the spectrum of industries and businesses, the common challenge experienced was "people." People are your single most important asset, but at times, can be your biggest challenge and the one you apportion a large percentage of your management time addressing. Hand over some responsibility to them; let them be part of the solution.

With the further development of technology, there will be newer and more scientific methods and systems and even programs that will look to finding new and more effective ways of managing people—managing their needs and improving their levels of engagement. In so doing, we may well decrease the gap between where the people are now and where we as managers want them to be. People are complex. They all think differently, all have different needs, see the world through their own eyes, and process this information in their own unique way!

As a manager in the middle, the technology, systems, and processes you have in your company are provided and facilitated from the powers that be. They are what they are, and you will be requested to use them. I don't suggest that all these programs are bad—not at all. Just don't let them turn you into a facilitator of information. You are the captain of the ship, and never underestimate the importance of your position as a manager in the middle. You are invaluable.

Build your own brand of management. Look for the ways you can hand the responsibility for repair over to your team. You can't do it for them. Technology can't manage people. You can.

In your own "business within a business" environment, you can start to do the small things very well all the time. It needs to start somewhere. Remove the clutter and rationally sift through and remove the complexities of the influences that surround you to enable you to reveal the answers that will naturally prevail through the simplicity of your own self-induced wisdom.

Keeping in step may be difficult to apply if it is on the far end of the scale from where you are now and what has become the norm in your business environment. How hard are you working, and how much time are you putting into your management of the BCE triangle: the BUSINESS, THE CUSTOMER, and the PEOPLE? One of the habits in Stephen Covey's book "The Seven Habits of Successful People" is "Sharpen the saw." It explains about a man who was too busy to stop cutting down a tree with his blunt saw because he said he did not have time to stop and sharpen it. But the reality is he would have had greater and quicker success had he taken the necessary time to sharpen the saw Don't be in too much of a hurry to get things done without taking the time to sharpen your skills.

I will leave you with this story:

A self-important college student was walking along the beach when he took it upon himself to stop and explain to a senior citizen resting on the steps why it was impossible for the older generation to understand his generation. "You grew up in a different world, actually, an almost primitive one," the student said. "The young people of today have grown up with television, jet planes, space travel, men walking on the moon, and we have nuclear energy, ships, smart phones, computers and sophisticated technology . . . and much more" After a brief silence, the senior citizen responded as follows. "You're right son. We did not have those things when we were young . . . so we invented them!"

What are you doing for the next generation? As a manager in the middle, what have you learned today, and what have you taught someone else? Your organization is a hungry beast that needs to be fed, and it is unfortunately all about the numbers. But there have to be checks and balances. I passionately believe there is room in your life as a manager to apply small and practical "keep in step" moments every day that will help you manage around the influences and turbulence of business today.

We are all under pressure to improve profitability. Margins are being squeezed; competition is increasing; cheaper imported goods are entering the market; shareholders demand better results; and the list goes on. Some or all of these things may be outside of your control but not your influence.

No interaction between customer or people in your business is complete without acknowledgement and recognition using these final words: **"Thank you for your business. It is most sincerely appreciated."**

Thank you for *your* business. In reading this book, you have delivered immeasurable value to me, and I hope in some small way it has changed the way you think, and in so doing will help you reinvent your wheel as it travels its path to achieving your goals and aspirations as a management leader.

"Opportunities are changing ceaselessly. Those who get there too early have gone too far, while those who get there too late cannot catch up. As the sun and the moon go through their courses, time does not go along with people. Therefore, sages do not value huge jewels as much as they value a little time. Time is hard to find and easy to lose."

Huainanzi—China. 2nd Century BC

Please review this book on Amazon if you found the ideas and concepts useful. I wish you every success in managing in the middle. What have you learned today, and what have you taught someone today?

You can contact me at - **thefixer953@gmail.com**

Website - **www.iainjohnston.co.za**

Facebook - **www.facebook.com/iainjohnston**

If you have learned something today and found any of THE FIXERS principles and ideas useful, please share them with a friend or colleague.

Acknowledgements and thanks for their advice and contribution to The Fixer

Justin Cohen - **http://www.justinpresents.com**

Jaco Brusse - **www.visualfabriq.com**

About the Author

Born in Scotland, and now based in South Africa, Iain Johnston is well known as a highly effective Management Consultant, Trainer, and Speaker with more than 30 years' experience at the sharp-end of management and business development.

Iain's passion is working in two critical business areas; Management Development, particularly junior and middle managers, where Iain and his team deliver high-value skills-based programs to accelerate management performance, and Employee Engagement, the key ingredient to ensure performance, productivity, and organisational effectiveness.

You can connect with Iain by e-mail at **thefixer953@gmail.com**, or on Social Media, via the links at the back of the book.

Made in the USA
Middletown, DE
12 September 2018